THE GREAT WAR THROUGH A DOUGHBOY'S EYES

THE GREAT WAR
THROUGH
A DOUGHBOY'S EYES

—⚡—

CORPORAL HOWARD P CLAYPOOLE'S DIARIES
AND LETTERS HOME FROM ENLISTMENT TO HIS
DISCHARGE AFTER WORLD WAR I

GREGORY S. VALLOCH

Charleston, SC
www.PalmettoPublishing.com

The Great War Through a Doughboy's Eyes
Copyright © 2022 by Gregory S. Valloch

Any errors or omissions in this book are mine and mine alone.

Hardcover ISBN: 978-1-68515-099-0
Paperback ISBN: 978-1-68515-533-9
eBook ISBN: 978-1-68515-534-6

IN MEMORIAM

Thank you, Professor Dennis Klinge, for instilling in me
a love of history and for teaching one of the best
courses on the Great War ever taught.

CONTENTS

Foreword · ix
Introduction · xi
Preface · xv
Chapter 1 The US Enters the War, Enlistment, and Mobilization
Training · 1
Chapter 2 Movement to France · 18
Chapter 3 Training in France · 25
Chapter 4 The German Spring Offensive of 1918 · · · · · · · · · · · · 37
Chapter 5 Wounding and Hospitalization · · · · · · · · · · · · · · · 42
Chapter 6 The Champagne-Marne Defensive · · · · · · · · · · · · · 59
Chapter 7 Meuse-Argonne Offensive · · · · · · · · · · · · · · · · · · 78
Chapter 8 The War Ends and Occupation Duty · · · · · · · · · · · · 82
Epilogue · 99
Acknowledgments · 146
Bibliography · 148
Glossary · 149
Notes · 151

MAPS
Fort Slocum · 5
Western Front, German Spring Offensive · · · · · · · · · · · · · · · · · · 39
Western Front, 3rd Division Front July 15-18, 1918 · · · · · · · · · · · · 62
Divisional Training Areas American Expeditionary Forces · · · · · · · 70
Plan of Attack of First Army · 74

APPENDIXES
1. International Order of Odd Fellows · · · · · · · · · · · · · · · · · · · 111
2. Howard Claypoole's Purple Heart Submission and Award · · · · · 113
3. Howard Claypoole's Purple Heart Order · · · · · · · · · · · · · · · 117

4. Howard Claypoole's Purple Heart Citation· · · · · · · · · · · · · · · 118
5. 6th Engineers Lineage and Honors· · · · · · · · · · · · · · · · · · · 119
6. Commendation from 1st Cavalry Division Commander· · · · · · · 124
7. Honorable Discharge with Enlistment Record · · · · · · · · · · · · 126
8. Five and Six Star Victory Ribbon Awards· · · · · · · · · · · · · · · 127
9. 3rd Division Military History · 130
10. Application for Headstone from the Veteran's Administration · 131
11. War Department Personnel Notification for Majel E.
    Claypoole· 132
12. Rifle Sling with Unit Insignia· 133
13. Trench Art German Shell · 134
14. French Bayonets· 135
15. German 10 Mark Gold Coin· 137
16. Application for Headstone· 138
17 Crests from Rifle Sling· 139

FOREWORD

This book that you have before you is perhaps one of the finest collections of an eyewitness account of the American side of World War I. The personal diary of Corporal Howard P. Claypoole (American Expeditionary Forces) provides the day-to-day observations from enlistment to recruit training to boarding a ship to cross the Atlantic Ocean and the brutal, inhuman battlefields of France.

The painstaking work of deciphering the over one-hundred-year-old diary and accompanying documents was performed by the author, Gregory Valloch, who is himself a retired colonel from the United States Army.

It is interesting to note that COL Valloch never met his grandfather but nonetheless went in search of him, through the letters he wrote home during World War I. Not only did COL Valloch find his grandfather in the diary and other letters he wrote, but he also gives Corporal Howard P. Claypoole life in these pages, as you read about the day-to-day activities and subsequent combat in France that he endured.

There are several points worth mentioning to the reader about this amazing collection.

The postcards and other letters he wrote to his parents from France took a month or more to get to their destination. Oftentimes parents didn't know if their son was even alive by the time they received the letters.

The letters, postcards, and the like from servicemen and -women were censored prior to being sent to the United States, so the effort to interpret those for this book was an extraordinary feat to determine the accuracy and validity that adds to the overall diary.

Folks "back home" didn't receive much news about the war on the radio or in newsreels from the movie theaters. Much like in World War II, that news was censored as well as not to alarm or frighten the populace.

Lastly, and maybe most important in the days in which we live now, it's important to remember that there are no "oh poor me" ruminations or diatribes within these pages. There are no "why are we here" or "what the hell are we doing" thoughts or feelings described within these pages.

Maybe those feelings aren't shared by Corporal Howard P. Claypoole in his diary or letters home because he knew, much like everyone else in politics and in the military, that America was there to "win" the war. How I wish we still had the same grit and determination and that same mentality today.

It was said that World War I was the "Great War" and the "War to End All Wars," and although that has proven to be far from the truth, this title was given to the worldwide conflict due to not only the utter brutality and horrendous casualties of the conflict but also the devastation of whole populations around the world.

This diary is one American soldier's view of that war. It's beautiful, it's simple as all beautiful things are, and it is deep and rich in its content, viewpoint, and experience.

I know you will enjoy getting to know Corporal Claypoole and seeing through his eyes what it was like to be a young, enthusiastic enlistee and walking with him across the muddy battlefields of World War I.

Mike Blackwood

INTRODUCTION

This project is my attempt to honor my maternal grandparents, Howard Percy Claypoole and Majel Elizabeth (Evans) Claypoole. I never knew my grandfather, and neither did my mother. My mother was born on November 21, 1939. My grandfather went in to the hospital for appendicitis in January 1940 and died in the hospital on January 17. Howard and Majel were operating a general store in Hartland, Vermont, at the time.

My grandparents had three children at the time of Howard's death: David Winfield Claypoole, Alice Jane Claypoole, and my mother, Patricia Louise Claypoole. My grandmother ended up selling the general store and eventually moving to Rutland, Vermont.

She never remarried.

As a child, I would go over to my grandmother's house in Rutland. It was a small one-story house with three bedrooms and an attic. The attic had a pull-down ladder, and I was often sent up to the attic to fetch certain things for my grandmother. In the attic hanging on a nail were two things that always caught my eye. There was an American World War I helmet with the 3rd Division patch painted on the front of it. There was also a rifle sling with unit crests from all kinds of foreign units. They included Australia, 2nd South African Infantry, T-8 Irish King's, RGA (Royal Garrison Artillery), the Royal Sussex Regiment, the Gloucestershire Regiment, the Black Watch (3rd Battalion, Royal Regiment of Scotland), the Prince of Wales' Own Regiment of Yorkshire, the 48th Highlanders of Canada, the Queen's Own Cameron Highlanders of Canada, and others. It all captured the imagination of a young boy. These crests stirred my interest in my grandfather and what he actually did in World War I.

I can't remember when I found out that my grandmother had my grandfather's diaries from World War I, but it had to have come up while I was a senior at Norwich University taking a course on World War I taught by Professor Dennis Klinge. I decided for my required research paper I would transcribe my grandfather's diaries from the war. I was also very fortunate that my grandmother had kept a lot of material that was my grandfather's. I had his enlistment papers, orders, citations, letters written home to his parents, dog tags, medals, coins, playing cards, dice, and discharge papers.

I also had his order awarding him a wound chevron that allowed me to apply, almost one hundred years later, for a well-earned Purple Heart. But that is a story for a later chapter.

I hope you enjoy this journey through World War I through the words of a young man who joined the army, became an engineer, and served his country honorably during the Great War.

FOR THE READER

The diaries were very small, and many words were abbreviated, sometimes making it difficult to understand what Howard was talking about. This work contains an acronym list at the end to help readers understand the context of what was written in the diaries. Also, if Howard misspelled a word in the diary, I did not correct the spelling. I transcribed the diaries exactly as they were written for historical accuracy.

PREFACE

Through the use of Howard Claypoole's diaries, paybook, letters, and postcards mailed home during the period of October 8, 1917, to August 29, 1919, I will try and recreate the life and hardships of an American enlisted man and his trials and tribulations while fighting the Germans to make the world safe for democracy.

There are two diaries that Howard Claypoole kept during the war and the period of occupation. The first diary covers the period from October 8, 1917, to October 5, 1918. This diary is three and one-quarter inches long and two inches wide, and on the cover are the words "Lest We Forget." There was a week's entry on every two facing pages. The writing is very small, sometimes smeared. Some entries were written in pen and other entries in pencil, and often they are very difficult to read without the use of a magnifying glass. The second diary has entries in it off and on from October 20, 1918, to August 29, 1919. This diary is six inches long and three inches wide. This material was easier to read and was not difficult to translate.

The letters and postcards I used were all mailed home to his mother and father, Mr. and Mrs. Winfield S. Claypoole. These letters and postcards numbered over sixty and were a good cross-reference with the diary, but because these letters were censored, they do not include much information that can be used to locate positions and/or battles. Some of his letters home were partially obliterated, erased, or had sections removed (censored words literally ripped out of the letter itself) because the information did not pass the censor's review (who was usually an officer in the regiment).

His paybook also had some information that was valuable to my research. Another source I used was *The American Heritage History of World War I*. This contained some information that helped me locate roughly where the 3rd Division was on the front. I also used many of Howard Claypoole's documents, orders, and other miscellaneous papers to get an insight of the times.

The writing of this book could not have been achieved without the help of Mrs. Howard P. Claypoole and my mother, Mrs. Patricia Claypoole Mitiguy.

CHAPTER 1

THE US ENTERS THE WAR, ENLISTMENT, AND MOBILIZATION TRAINING

The United States of America did not want to go to war in Europe. But the sinking of the USS *Lusitania* was the final straw tied to the German policy of unrestricted submarine warfare in the Atlantic Ocean. This finally pushed the United States over the edge and into the war.

> On April 2nd, 1917, President Woodrow Wilson addressed Congress, asking for a declaration of war against Germany. ...Two days after Wilson's speech, the Senate overwhelmingly declared that a state of war existed between Germany and the United States. Two days later the House of Representatives followed suit. The United States had entered "the Great War."[1]

Howard Percy Claypoole was born on January 30, 1893, in Bridgeton, Hope Township, Warren County, New Jersey, the son of Winfield Scott Claypoole and Jane M. Dawson Claypoole. The Claypoole family can be traced back to his tenth great-grandfather John Claypoole, who was born in King's Cliffe, Northamptonshire, England, in 1508. Howard's mother, Jane Dawson, can be traced back to her great-great-great-great-grandfather John Dawson, born about 1716 in Great Bardfield in Essex, England.

WINFIELD SCOTT CLAYPOOLE WITH HIS WIFE, ANN DAWSON CLAYPOOLE,
AND HIS SONS, CLARENCE AND HOWARD, CIRCA 1908 (PHOTOGRAPH
COURTESY OF ELRIC JOHNSTON, GRANDSON OF HOWARD CLAYPOOLE).

EARLY UNITED STATES ARMY RECRUITING POSTER.

It is unknown if Howard Claypoole saw the poster above or another poster asking for young men to join the army. There were six months between the declaration of war by the United States and Howard Claypoole's enlistment. Unfortunately, I do not know why it took six months for him to enlist. But enlist he did.

When Howard enlisted into the regular army, he was single and twenty-four years old. Not much is known about Howard's upbringing, the schools he attended, or his life before he entered the army. His enlistment record (see Appendix 7) states he enlisted on October 9, 1917, in Atlantic City, New Jersey. His profession listed on his enlistment record states: "Knowledge of any vocation: R. R. [Railroad] Agent." His enlistment record also states that he enlisted, and the word "inducted" is scratched through, meaning he was not drafted. This chapter begins with the start of Howard Claypoole's diaries. This is where his journey began as a soldier in the United States Army.

—⟋⟍—

Monday, 8 October 1917- Left Atlantic City 9:15 am. Arrive at Fort Slocum[1] 4:50 p.m. Had mess, a slight exam. Went to show, took a shower and retired.

9 Oct.- Crawled out at 6 bells had mess. Went through more exam, vaccinated, inoculated, received part of clothing, assigned barracks, retired at 9pm.

---

1 Fort Slocum, New York, was a US military post that occupied David's Island in the western end of Long Island Sound in the city of New Rochelle, New York, from 1867 to 1965. After the American entry into World War I, Fort Slocum became one of the busiest recruit training stations in the country, processing one hundred thousand soldiers per year and serving as the recruit examination station for soldiers from New York, New Jersey, Pennsylvania, and the New England states. Between 1917 and 1919, over 140,000 recruits passed through the post. In fact, Recruit Week in December 1917 brought so many recruits to Fort Slocum that an overflow had to be housed in New Rochelle. ("Fort Slocum," Wikipedia, https://en.wikipedia. org/wiki/Fort_Slocum, accessed November 4, 2021)

10 Oct.- Up at 5 am., given the morning to get a haircut. Loafed the rest of day, went to YMCA at night and took in shows.

11 Oct.- Up at 5 am. Drilled all morning. Went in mess hall 3 pm to work, out at 8:30 p.m. Some Day! Hit the hay 9:30 p.m.

12 Oct.- Up at 5 a.m. went right to work in mess hall had 10 min. for a smoke at noon out at 3 p.m. Played cards at night rained at night

13 Oct.- Up at 4:30 a.m. Drilled all morning. Had inspection just before noon. Received mess kits and went to football game in afternoon.

—m—

A rough estimate of the size of the camp can be arrived at through information mailed home in a letter on October 13, 1917: "I had to wait on tables, prepare dishes get food all the soups and Vegitables [sic] are put 4 big Battleships and that serves the whole Table, twenty two people at each table and fourty [sic] eight tables in Mess Hall this place feeds perhaps one fifth of the people in the place."[2]

FORT SLOCUM, DAVID'S ISLAND, NEW YORK.
LOCATED CLOSE TO NEW ROCHELLE, NEW YORK.

The size of the camp was approximately five thousand men. Wake-up time was usually at 5:00 a.m. The first week at Slocum was occupied by drilling, inspections, examinations, and drawing some equipment and clothing.

—∿—

Notes- Got a beautiful cold during the weeks performance.

14 Oct.- Roamed around the Island not much doing. Fried chicken and ice cream for eats.

15 Oct.- Drilled in morning, examinations, informed of departure – turned in all but one blank[et].

—∿—

At this point, Howard seemed to enjoy the army life, as exemplified in this letter dated October 15, 1917: "The 21 Company is all filled up so we had to join the 26th Company. I don't know exactly where I am yet. If you ask or try and find out they don't tell you anything. All I know is that I am in the Army and having a good time so far."[3]

—∿—

16 Oct.- Left Fort Slocum 9:00 a.m. Left Jersey City 11:45 am arrive North Philadelphia 2;20 p.m. Red Cross gave apples and cigarettes. Arrive at barracks[2] 8:00 p.m.

—∿—

---

2 This is Washington Barracks in the vicinity of Washington, DC. The 1st Battalion is noted in *The Sixth Engineer History* to be quartered in Washington Barracks.

He was stationed at the Washington Barracks, Washington DC. At these barracks, the sleeping quarters were better than at Fort Slocum: "Our place here is a lot better than Fort Slocum we sleep in tents 8 in each eat with mess kits we don't get as much to eat as we did at Slocum but we get filled up."[4]

—∿—

17 Oct.- Drilled all morning got O.D's [Olive Drab Uniforms] in afternoon, visited Y.M.C.A. at night retired.

18 Oct.- Drilled all day, parade at 4:30 p.m. Mess and day is over. Write letters at night.

19 Oct.- Drilled all morning, tieing [sic] knots in afternoon, rained later at night. Telling stories in tent at night

20 Oct.- Drilled in morning, received second inoculation and got guns. Parade in afternoon

21 Oct.- Did big wash and layed [sic] around in morning. Football game in afternoon. Dull evening

22 Oct.- Drill in morning same in afternoon. Went up town at night to burlesque. Had coat altered

23 Oct.- Lots of drilling, parade, Went to entertainment and dance at night got soaking wet coming home.

24 Oct.- Cold and rainy, took half mile run. Nothing doing in afternoon.

25 Oct.- Drill hard all day up town at night, left "Independent Order of Odd Fellows" I.O.O.F. charm for engraving. Retired early.

26 Oct.- Busy day and fair eats. Got I.O.O.F charm at night. Numerous jokes exchanged before Taps.

27 Oct.- One drill in morning. Assigned as camp orderly for day. Had big eats up town at night. Went to movies and movies and to gaiety then returned.

28 Oct.- Went to Methodist Church in morning had dinner in church parlor. Wrote letters in eve.

29 Oct.- Rain all day, inoculated in morning, stuck close to tent took walk at night and washed clothes

30 Oct.- Heavy drill all day to[o] wet for Parades, stayed in and retired early.

31 Oct.- Heavy drill, received box from Edgar and Florence, had to stay in. Saloons closing at 12 midnight

Thursday, 1 November, 1917- Drilled all day, Parade, went up town at night with Joe.

2. Nov.- Drill all day. Had show at Y.M.C.A. in evening

3 Nov.- Slight drill, parade, get ready for leave to Rifle range In the city at night

At Washington Barracks, all companies fell out for parades on the parade ground every Tuesday and Thursday. Majors and captains rode horses, lieutenants led companies, and the band played at these retreat parades. October 25, 1917, was the first parade with weapons. While Howard was at Washington Barracks, drill took up a considerable amount of his time.

Sunday was basically a relaxation day. Some of the nightly excursions in Washington included going to a burlesque, dancing, visiting saloons, and going to the Gaiety Theatre. He also went with some of his buddies to the Methodist church on Sundays for dinners put on by the church.

—⟋⟋⟍—

4 Nov.- Left for Belvoir VA.[3] 10;00 a.m. arrive 11;30 a.m. Some place, took pictures in P.M.

—⟋⟋⟍—

On November 4, his unit left for Fort Belvoir for marksmanship training in the morning and moved by boat down the Potomac to Belvoir, which was about an hour and a half journey.

---

3 "The post (Fort Belvoir) was founded during World War I as Camp A. A. Humphreys, named for American Civil War Union Army General Andrew A. Humphreys, who was also Chief of Engineers....Camp Humphreys was established in World War I as the U.S. Army Engineers Training School. It served as the post-graduate institution for U.S. Military Academy engineers and a finishing school for engineering troops headed to war." ("Fort Belvoir, Wikipedia, https://en.wikipedia.org/wiki/Fort_Belvoir, accessed November 5, 2021) It is interesting that Howard Claypoole only calls it Fort Belvoir and not Camp Humphries.

HOWARD CLAYPOOLE WITH TENTMATES, WASHINGTON BARRACKS, WASHINGTON, DC, OCTOBER 1917. HOWARD IS FRONT ROW, BOTTOM RIGHT.

HOWARD CLAYPOOLE WITH TENTMATES, WASHINGTON BARRACKS, WASHINGTON, DC, OCTOBER 1917. HOWARD IS ON THE FAR LEFT BETWEEN THE STACKED RIFLES' BAYONETS.

THE TENTS AT WASHINGTON BARRACKS WHERE THE
SIXTH ENGINEERS ENCAMPED IN OCTOBER 1917.

HOWARD AND OTHER TENTMATES. RIFLES AT STACK ARMS WITH BAYONETS.
EVERYONE IS WEARING CARTRIDGE BELTS, CAMPAIGN HATS, AND LEGGINGS.

HOWARD CLAYPOOLE WITH TENTMATES, WASHINGTON BARRACKS, WASHINGTON, DC, OCTOBER 1917. HOWARD IS ON THE FAR LEFT, WITHOUT CAMPAIGN HAT.

HOWARD CLAYPOOLE AT WASHINGTON BARRACKS, OCTOBER 1917. NOTE THE CAMPAIGN HAT, TIE, AND LEGGINGS.

This is a photograph of Company B, 6th Engineers taken on October 31, 1917, at Washington Barracks, Washington DC. Howard Claypoole is in the front row, fourth from the right (photograph courtesy of Kathleen Claypoole, granddaughter of Howard P. Claypoole).

—m—

5 Nov.- Went to rifle[4] range for practice, good day had lots of fun.

—⚭—

The targets that they shot at were stationary targets that looked like the head and shoulders of a man. Five points was the highest possible score for a shot. Howard wrote home in a letter some more details about his time on the rifle range:

> The shooting was all slow fire at 200-300-500 and 600 yds the best in our company made 163 out of a possible 200. I made 140. One of my chums made 20. We shoot prone, kneeling and sitting. We shot again Wednesday all rapid fire 10 shots in 60 sec. I made 107 out of 150 in that.

Howard also stated in this letter home, "It looks like a dime at 600 yds.[5]"

—⚭—

6. Nov.- Had stable duty, skipped out after dinner and loafed.

7 Nov.- Shot rapid fire[5] on range all day made fair average.

8 Nov.- In butts all day, worked phone in afternoon, went to Y.M.C.A. show at night

9. Nov.- Had rapid fire in morning and the afternoon off

---

4 "The M1903 Springfield, officially the United States Rifle, Caliber .30-06, Model 1903, is an American five-round magazine-fed, bolt-action service repeating rifle, used primarily during the first half of the 20th century...and it was officially adopted by the United States as the standard infantry rifle on June 19, 1903 where it saw service in World War I." ("M1903 Springfield," Wikipedia, https://en.m.wikipedia.org/wiki/M1903_Springfield, accessed December 8, 2021)
5

10 Nov.- Shot for record and made hell of a poor one.

—◊◊◊—

11 Nov.- Left Belvoir and back to Washington barracks. All tired out but able to eat.

12 Nov.- Drilled all day, had bath first in 10 days, cold water and almost froze.

13 Nov.- Drill in morning, dug trenches in afternoon in Virginia up town at night.

14 Nov.- Drill in morning. Rowing in afternoon, waiter besides.

15 Nov.- Drill in morning. All drills off for P.M. to town at night. Frank broke quarantine.

16 Nov. Load cars at P.R.R. station all day till 6:30 p.m. Some day, write letters at night.

17 Nov.- Drill in morning. Parade and inspection in afternoon. Went to show at night.

18 Nov.- Layed [sic] around camp and scouted the town for a photographer

19 Nov.- Drill in morning, out in boats in afternoon, up town at night.

20. Nov.- Drill in morning, drew clothing in afternoon, up town at night.

21 Nov.- Took hike and worked about camp.

22 Nov.- Drilled in morning, camp detail in afternoon, up town at night.

23 Nov.- Took hike and worked about camp.

24 Nov.- Parade, inspection and hike. Left for home on 7:00 train arrive 12:00 midnight

25 Nov.- At home and to Atlantic City, left at 9:00 p.m. arrive at barracks 5:00 a.m.

26 Nov.- Arrive from home no drill all day, retired early.

27 Nov. Drill in morning, camp detail in afternoon, downtown to Y.M. at night

28 Nov.- Dull day, snow and rain, layed [*sic*] around

29 Nov.- Went to Mount Rainier [Maryland] and for dinner had turkey at barracks. 6:30 to dance at night.

—␣—

For Thanksgiving, Howard went to Mt. Rainier (Maryland) for dinner after receiving tickets from the YMCA. A turkey dinner was served, and upon their return to the barracks, a big supper of turkey and fixings was served to the men. Howard always seems to mention how good the food was in his diary. I believe he was quite happy with the Thanksgiving meals he had on Thanksgiving Day, 1917.

—␣—

30 Nov.- Rainy, not much doing, wrote letters, told stories

Saturday, 1 December 1917- Parade and inspection, gates locked at night, stayed in and told stories.

The 3rd Division history confirms the parade and inspection: "On Saturday, December 1st, the regiment was inspected by the commanding officer, Colonel Harts. Every officer and man was required to be fully equipped and ready to leave."[6]

Pvt. Howard Claypoole's first two months in the army were spent learning how to be a soldier. Drilling is the predominant activity listed in his diary. Drilling instills discipline in men and imbues in them the necessity to follow commands quickly and efficiently. There are also parades and inspections and issuing of uniforms and equipment.

He also went to Fort Belvoir for marksmanship training with the 1903 Springfield rifle. His first day at the range, he specifically notes that he had fun that day. On another day, he worked in "the butts" all day. This is where men would raise and lower targets and indicate on a target where the round struck the target—not quite the automated target and scoring system used today. You can tell that he was not happy with just qualifying as a marksman by his comment "shot for record and made hell of a poor one."

His entry on November 12 is telling of how often he was allowed to utilize facilities to conduct personal hygiene and have the opportunity to take a bath: "had bath first in 10 days, cold water and almost froze." This and other posts in the diary I believe give a sense of who Howard Claypoole was. He never really complained; he seemed like he was happy to take a bath although he almost froze while taking it.

After he returned from Fort Belvoir, some of the entries include what I would call engineer specific training. He dug trenches and went out in boats, and this is where drill turns into hiking, commonly called "road marching" in today's vernacular. Road marching is a great conditioner to toughen men and allow them to be moved around the battlefield quickly and efficiently. All their road marching done will pay off in the future.

CHAPTER 2

MOVEMENT TO FRANCE

The movement of the American Expeditionary Force (AEF) to Europe was the first time the United States deployed an army overseas. It was a monumental task to move men and material overseas, establish training areas, and prepare to assist the British and French in fighting the Germans. The scope of this had never before been attempted in the history of the United States. Civilian leadership did not understand the complexities of this entire operation. This is clear in the guidance that the Secretary of War (now called the Secretary of Defense) gave to General Pershing. "Before [General] Pershing departed for France, Secretary [of War] Baker told him: 'I will give you only two orders, one to go to France, and the other to come home. In the meantime, your authority in France will be supreme.'"[7]

Over there, over there
Send the word, send the word over there
That the Yanks are coming, the Yanks are coming!
And we won't come back till it's over over there.[8]

Orders are the method in which the army authorizes movement for units and individuals. And so it was for the 6th Engineer Regiment that received the following order.

POST OF WASHINGTON BARRACKS, DC

Special Orders

No. 236

December 2, 1917

Pursuant to instructions contained in telegram, Headquarters Eastern Department, dated November 14 1917, the 6th Regiment of Engineers, consisting of fifty (50) officers and 1,583 enlisted men, will proceed by rail from Washington Barracks, DC, to Hoboken, NJ, reporting upon arrival to the commanding officer. The Quartermaster Corps will furnish the necessary transportation.

The travel directed is necessary in the military service

BY ORDER OF COLONEL HARTS:
W. Mel. Wolfe
Captain, Engineers USR
Adjutant[9]

—ɷ—

2 Dec.-Broke camp ready at noon, leave at 7:15 p.m. Sat with guards, leave station 7:15 PM: eat with guards – leave sta[tion] about 9 PM ride all night.

—ɷ—

The Sixth Engineer history adds some detail to the movement from Washington Barracks:

Towards evening the regiment was formed by battalions near the flagpole on the parade ground. Check roll-call was held for all organizations, arms and equipment were stacked, and the regiment waited for final orders to move. At 6:00 o'clock the bugles sounded, and to the music of the Engineer Band the regiment marched out through the big iron gates of Washington Barracks.[10]

—⁂—

3 Dec. Pull in sta[tion] at J. City 4 Am. leave at 7: A.m. arr Hoboken 9:30- a.m. load right on Geo Wash.[6] on guard most of the night.

—⁂—

The *George Washington* was a large ship, and it was not only carrying part of the 6th Engineer Regiment, but it also had an assortment of generals, laborers, nurses, and other branches of service on board: "The USS *George Washington* was also carrying casual officers, several major generals, about five thousand negro labor troops, medical and quartermaster troops, and sixty-five nurses."[11]

—⁂—

4 Dec.- Look about ship visit sailors quarters eat at 9:30 a.m. and 3:30 p.m. Poker games. Leave dock 10:15 P.M.

---

6 "SS *George Washington* was an ocean liner built in 1908 for the Bremen-based Norddeutscher Lloyd (a German shipping company) and was named after George Washington, the first president of the United States. The ship was also known as USS *George Washington* (ID-3018) and USAT *George Washington* in service of the United States Navy and United States Army, respectively, during World War I…In total, she carried 48,000 passengers to France and returned 34,000 to the United States after the Armistice. *George Washington* also carried US President Woodrow Wilson to France twice for the Paris Peace Conference." ("SS George Washington," Wikipedia, https://en.m.wikipedia.org/wiki/SS_George_Washington, accessed December 1, 2021)

—◊◊◊—

The Sixth Engineer history provides some more detail on the departure:

> At 11:00 o'clock the *George Washington* slipped its moorings and proceeded slowly down the harbor followed by the Huron [another transport carrying more of the [6th Engineers]. The morning of the 5th found the two transports escorted by the battleship *Montana*[7] and one torpedo-boat destroyer, out of sight of land, started a voyage that was to last sixteen days.[12]

—◊◊◊—

5 Dec.- Sent on guard 1 P.M. 2 hr on 4 off until next day.

6 Dec.- On guard until 1 P.M. given tobacco by Red Cross. Storm rough sea-sick. One lost off Battleship <u>found</u>

7 Dec.- Still rough still sick on guard couldn't eat. Hang on rails slide down stairs, good for a movie.

—◊◊◊—

The Sixth Engineer history adds an interesting item about the target practice conducted a few days after leaving port: "The target practice of the gun crews was watched with great interest by all aboard. The battleship

---

7 "USS *Montana* (ACR-13/CA-13), also referred to as 'Armored Cruiser No. 13,' later renamed *Missoula* and reclassified CA-13, was a Tennessee-class armored cruiser of the United States Navy. She was built by the Newport News Drydock & Shipbuilding Co.; her keel was laid down in April 1905, she was launched in December 1906, and she was commissioned in July 1908. The final class of armored cruisers to be built for the US Navy, *Montana* and her sisters were armed with a main battery of four ten-inch (254 mm) guns, and were capable of a top speed of 22 knots (41 km/h; 25 mph)." ("USS Montana (ACR-13)," Wikipedia, https://en.m.wikipedia.org/wiki/USS_Montana_(ACR-13), accessed December 8, 2021)

[USS *Montana*] would tow a target, at which the two transports directed their fire. The accuracy of this was indeed gratifying to the men."[13]

Excerpts from the personal log books of US Navy patriot Dewitt T. McGill (1917–1919) on board the USS *George Washington* note that he liked the amenities on board:

> Left Hoboken NJ for France, we are not told where exactly. The *George* is well equipped with all conveniences such as telephones, speaking tubes, elevators, pianos, Victrolas, and a daily newspaper printed on a board call the "Hatchet" which gives the latest war and sporting news daily.[14]

—⁂—

8 Dec.- Come off guard 1 P.M. still sick rough water eat 1 sandwich 2 orange 1 apple at night sleep well after fresh air on deck. Destroyer captures Austrian boat

9 Dec.- calmer although windy feel better eat well, enjoy fresh air. On guard at 5 P.M. to[o] hot for comfort

10 Dec.- Leave post 1 A.M. go to galley to get big feed get souv[enir] spoon. Had great time with sheff [Chef]. to[o] hot to sleep

11 Dec.- Bum eats Joe and I have good talk on Deck. On guard 5 P.M. still hot

12 Dec.- On guard. down in galley 2 A.M. had eats nice day Bought Watch $3.00 Target practice

13 Dec.- Sold Watch $7.00 see porpoise. Birds also. Inspection arms. Gets colder. On guard Starboard Aft. Eat in galley

14 Dec.- On guard cold, wear overcoat. Ven. Inspec[tion]. Cloudy, part rain water rough

15 Dec.- Nice day, cool, pick up 6 destroyers, Battleship goes back. Eat hot bread at 2:A.M. Sun after coming off guard.

16 Dec.- Stormy, Sea rough, pick up 7 or 8 more Destroyers boat rolls. Sit on garbage can and have hair cut. Life Boats battered and lost

—◊◊◊—

The History of the Sixth Engineers addresses the storm and how some soldiers were lost:

> The storm grew worse all that day and into the night. The waves were large enough to sweep across the deck of even as large a ship as the George Washington…C Company was on guard and had a post at the stern in a small deck house covering a machine gun. As the corporal of the guard was visiting the post a high wave broke over the ship, tearing away this deck house, and washing overboard Corporal Kehl and Private Smith of C Company. Although these men, equipped with their life belts, were seen struggling in the waves, the storm was still too severe to make any attempt at rescue possible.[15]

—◊◊◊—

17 Dec.- 8 Guards washed over, no one allowed on deck all day. Several hurt in Mess Hall grub flying all over. Lighthouses spotted.

18 Dec.- Heavy gale, allowed out at noon, Sailor and Soldier picked up by Destroyer Travel slow in circle 4 mi. change in time, not so rough

19 Dec.- Good day. Tramp ship[8] off starboard on guard at night other t[rans]'port Leave. (Airplanes greet us)

20 Dec.- See land about 11:15 A. M. Enter River B. Great sight, big Forts Boat stops at 12:30 P.M. Think Porpeous [porpoise] Submarine. French come in row boats to greet us.

21 Dec.- Still on ship girls flock around in rowboats, soldiers drop them coin get piece of pie after breakfast. Coons unload cargo on Tugs.

—ᶆ—

The History of the Sixth Engineers addresses the small boats selling goods to the soldiers:

> During the delay between the arrival and debarkation the transports were surrounded by a multitude of small boats selling fruits and pastries. After the voyage the chance to buy almost anything was welcomed, especially the chance to get fruit; consequently the small boats, each with one or two Brittany women on board, did a lively business. These people dressed in very queer caps, large, loose garments, and wodden [sic] shoes, were at the time very novel and interesting to all.[16]

---

8 "A boat or ship engaged in the tramp trade is one which does not have a fixed schedule or published ports of call." ("Tramp Trade," Wikipedia, https://en.m.wikipedia.org/wiki/Tramp_trade, accessed November 15, 2021)

CHAPTER 3

TRAINING IN FRANCE

The composition of a division in World War I was quite different from a division today. Divisions could actually have different compositions based on missions. According to the 3rd Division history, this was the organization of the division as it deployed to France:

> A full Infantry Division is, roughly speaking, composed of 27,000 men and is commanded by a Major General. Included in this organization are two Infantry Brigades of two Infantry Regiments and one Machine Gun Battalion each, and an Artillery Brigade of three regiments, two lights (75's) and one heavy (6" Howitzer). Then there are, for their respective special duties, a regiment of Engineers, a battalion of Signal troops, and a Divisional Machine Gun Battalion (motorized). Each brigade has its headquarters, consisting of the Brigadier-General commanding, and the personnel of his staff and assistants. The Division Headquarters Staff numbers approximately 50 officers and 126 men. To complete the division, add the Headquarters Troop, Train Headquarters, Military Police Company, Supply, Sanitary, Engineer and Ammunition Trains, the Mobile Ordnance Repair Shops, Mobile Veterinary Section, Division Salvage Squad, Railhead Unit, Clothing and Bathing Unit, Mobile Field Laboratory, Sales Commissary, Machine Shop Truck Units, a Bakery

Company and a Laundry Company. Each and every unit, whether combatant, or otherwise, has its own particular function and duties and its efficient operation and performance of duty is essential to the success of the Division as a whole.[17]

After three years of war and horrendous casualties, the French people were very enthusiastic about the arrival of the American Expeditionary Forces.

As the bulk of the division settled into its new home to learn the basics of soldiering, the French authorities persuaded Pershing to allow a battalion of the 16th Infantry to march through Paris on the Fourth of July to encourage the French people with the appearance of American troops. The parade culminated at Picpus Cemetery, burial place of Gilbert du Montier, the Marquis de Lafayette. At the tomb of the American Revolution hero, on behalf of Pershing, Col. Charles E. Stanton, a quartermaster officer fluent in French, gave a rousing speech, ending with the words "Lafayette, we are here!" Mistakenly attributed to Pershing, the words nevertheless captured the sentiment of many Americans repaying an old debt.[18]

NOTE: As soon as the troops reached France, the letters home were censored. Portions of the letters were erased, obliterated with a heavy black marker, or ripped out. The names of towns and villages in France were taken from his diary.

—ɷ—

22 Dec.- Leave ship land at Brest[9] 2:30 P.M. Leave 6:30 P.M. after hike through City, drink of Wine a little French bread, in Box cars no heat 35 in a car. travel all night little sleep.

23 Dec.- Arr[ive] at Laval 7:30 A.M. Get coffee ride on very cold ground covered with snow scenery great

24 Dec.- Still in Bx Cars land at Troys 10:30 A.m. Very cold go on arr[ive] at Paruthoy 11:30 P.M. Sleep in deserted house on floor 12:30

25 Dec.- Get up 11:00 A.M. Bad headache drink champaign [*sic*] and varities of wine in hotel had first mess at night headache didn't eat.

26 Dec.- up at 6:30 few exercises unload cars took hike change quarters spend night at hotel. Wash feet

27 Dec.- Take all morn hike in Snow storm Another hike in afternoon get stuff from Bk. Bg [barracks bag]. At night visit Hotel.

28 Dec.- Snow hard most of Day hike haul wood. Cold all day. At hotel at night go to bed shoes freeze.

29 Dec.- Cold snow a little get wood all day get mail of Dec 1st and 2nd our first mail go to Barber at night Snow all week shoes wet all week

30 Dec.- Go to next town visit G. Co. get chocolate get potatoe ½ for dinner cold visit Hotel retire early

---

9 "In 1917, during the First World War, Brest was used as the disembarking port for many of the troops coming from the United States. Thousands of such men came through the port on their way to the front lines. The United States Navy established a naval air station on 13 February 1918 to operate seaplanes. The base closed shortly after the Armistice of 11 November 1918." ("Brest, France," Wikipedia, https://en.m.wikipedia.org/wiki/Brest,_France, accessed December 8, 2021)

31 Dec.- Get wood in morning get slice of bread for dinner muster in afternoon have eats and drink at Hotel at night Get up 3 min of 12 everything quiet

1 January 1918 (Tuesday)- Haul wood all day sign pay roll feel bum get pills from Frank.

2 Jan.- Ear[ache]. Get wood go to Hospital eat jam and write letter

3. Jan.- Special duty with Lacomb. Feel bum. Cold. Visit Frank and Joe at night some smoke

4 Jan.- out in woods all day see airopla[ne]. Hear big guns go to hospital at night

5 Jan.- Hike in morning. Same in afternoon get first butter. Joe and Frank move in [to] our shack. Go to hotel

6 Jan.- No Revelrie [reveille] inspection at 11:00 A.m. good chow wash handkerchiefs

7 Jan.- Took hike and haul wood snow and cold part rain bum day get all wet

8 Jan.- Snow all day hike to Vaux get chocolate. Short hike in afternoon.

9 Jan.- Go to woods all day get wine (sick) come back

10 Jan.- On guard didn't shave so put on wood pile all day Frank leaves

11 Jan.- Go woods all day get freight from Depot and go to Hospital for ear lay around at night

12.- Jan.- on guard go to Hospital rain and snow Joe and I have feed at 10:30 P.M. Peas bread sheese [*sic*] and sugar

13 Jan.- Come off guard 8:30 A.M. raining. Good chow noon canteen opens get French book

14 Jan.- On detail at station get P.A. Go to Chassigny with chow French wagon train help us

15 Jan.- On detail at sta. cut wood keep fire in Library shave and have toast

16 Jan.- On guard rain all day and night have feed at night

17.- Off guard work at sta in morning go to woods in afternoon have toast retire

18 Jan.- Loading detail cart lumber unload and pile. Helped sort squad boxes

19 Jan.- Go to woods clean shack 61 -Get paid at noon (100F 10C.) all up to Hotel but Joe and I.

[NOTE: While in France Howard was paid in French Francs and centimes.]

20 Jan.- Nice day have good chow. Go to Vaux in afternoon get choc. At Hotel in evening

21 Jan.- On loading detail go to woods in afternoon Joe and I at Hotel in eve. Take <u>bath</u>

22 Jan.- On guard have good eats rain at night 3rd plat'. Go away

23 Jan.- Come off guard work on Barn in afternoon

24 Jan.- Go to woods in morning unload cars in afternoon nice day warm.

25 Jan.- Help load wagons work on Barn in afternoon Go to Hotel at night

26 Jan.- Go to woods in morning work on Barn in afternoon Go to Hotel at night have eats and retire

27 Jan.- Inspection have good chow unload cars and rec'd 6 letters

28 Jan.- Work on Barn all day J[o]e and I have eats at night mice noisie [*sic*]

29 Jan.- On loading detail in morning work on Barn in afternoon

30 Jan.- Loading detail work on Barn feed. Mice run on face at night.

31 Jan.- On guard all day and night. Nice day very foggy Eats at night

During January, in the diary there are hikes, work details, and the mentioning of "going to woods." There is no indication of what this entailed. It may have been to haul wood, or it may have been tactics practiced in the woods. There was the loading of wagons and railroad cars and carpentry work. Howard was disciplined in January for not shaving and was put on the woodpile all day.

Friday, 1 February 1918- Learn of Will Hastings death of (31st) work on loading detail all day.

2 Feb.- Go to woods cart wood all day Part of the 26th Eng come in Have eats at night.

3 Feb.- Move up over kitchen have inspection good feed

4 Feb.- Go to woods in morning work on Barn in afternoon

5 Feb.- On loading detail 9 aeroplanes pass Joe and I have lunch at night

6 Feb.- Bostwick and Frank return on loading detail all day

7 Feb.- Get paid 102 F. 50 C. Super on guard. Get helmets and gas masks

8 Feb.- Have gas test bummed around most of the day draw 100 rounds of ammunition

9 Feb.- Super. Guard start to pack many soused scrap at night and crap games

10 Feb.- Leave Prauthoy 12:30 travel day and night get to mi[le] of Paris in morning travel on scenery great

11 Feb.- stop of at Le Bourget and by [*sic*] wine and beer travel on arr at Daingt at dark sleep on ground

12 Feb.- Leave in Eng[lish] trucks 9 A. M. about 6 mi from the front go to Voyennes on same line from front

13 Feb.- Tare [*sic*] down old structure of bridge same all day rain come through roof at night.

—ɯ—

The History of the Sixth Engineers provides more detail on the bridges under construction: "On the 13th the detachment of one hundred twenty men from Company B, under the command of Lieutenant T. J. Allen, went in lorries to Voyennes to start work on heavy steel bridges over the Somme river and the canal."[19]

—m—

14. Feb.- Work on tool house all day Eng[lish] hardtack and tea for eats Bye [sic] coat and drink with Eng. At night.

15 Feb.- Room orderly Gerries come over at night put out light bombs shake building strike next town

16 Feb.- Go to Nestle[10] [Nesle] bomb struck Eng quarters kill 26 strike other houses there the night before. Go through dugout. Fellows leave me walk home alone air rade [sic] at night

17 Feb.- Provo Guard Inspection in afternoon change quarters

18 Feb.- Went to Nesle work all day. Go again at night work till 10 P.M. hike all the way

19 Feb.- Go to Nestle [sic] all day bye [sic] cheese bread and jam. Bye [sic] shoes 8F. Tommie steel shoes

20 Feb.- Go to Nestle [sic]. Charlie and I have steak and feed at night

21 Feb.- Work on bridge all day have feed at night

22 Feb.- Work on Bridge. Go on stone pile in afternoon Charlie and I have eats at night

23 Feb.- Work on Bridge and stone pile, good day have eats at night

---

10 Work on all bridges went slowly owing to the lack of special tools, particularly wrenches. The morning of March 21, however, saw all the bridges completed with the exception of one at Béthincourt and one on the outskirts of Nesle.

24 Feb.- Work in morning have bath in P.M. and Inspection got letter from Joe and Barb

25. Feb.- Work from 2 P.M. till 10 P.M. sec schift [*sic*] get eats after work.

26 Feb.- Work sec shift on Bridge things the same a little rain at night

27 Feb.- Sleep till noon Work on Bridge Lots of fireing [*sic*] on front

28 Feb.- Rec. Box from home and Watch. Two letter from Jo. Work on Bridge

—⚏—

In February, the company prepared for combat action. They drew gas masks and helmets, and there is a mention of a gas test, and they also drew one hundred rounds of ammunition. On the tenth of February, they left Prauthoy and maneuvered to within one mile of Paris. Howard traveled through Le Bourget, Paunat, and Voyennes, which was about six miles from the front. This part of the front was held by British troops. Howard mentions riding in English trucks, eating English food, and drinking with the English at night. The 6th Engineers were moved because the commander of the British Fifth Army needed to reinforce his thin line against the upcoming German offensive:

> The 6th, 12th and 14th US Engineer regiments had been rushed forward to help the Fifth Army, and [General Sir Hubert] Gough was intensely proud of them. They had built their bridges just in time to prepare them for demolition. After that, they would fight with the shattered Fifth as infantry, the first American troops to know full scale battle since the Civil War.[20]

The bridges mentioned by Howard Claypoole and the bridges mentioned in the Sixth Engineer history were hastily built and were the same bridges that Gough talks about being prepared for demolition. The bridges were built to continue the offensive toward Germany. The attack by the Germans then required the bridges to be prepared for demolition, so the Germans could not get across the Marne River and continue their attack toward Paris

—៷៷—

Friday 1 March 1918- Sleep till noon Snow in quarters everything wet. Work on bridge

2 Mar.- Sleep late work on bridge Frank burned, rain and snow. fighting close to work

3 Mar.- Work from 10 A.M. till 2 P.M. inspec at 4:30 P.M. eats 6:30 P.M. Cold and wet.

4 Mar.- Work on bridge from 5 A.M. till 2 P.M. Snow all day very cold. Cut B's Hair

5 Mar.- Work on bridge near Nestle [sic] go to Nestle [sic] with Luitenant [sic] snow in Morning

6 Mar.- Work on Bridge nice day get letter from Home

7 Mar.- Work on Bridge nice day Get paid. Bye [sic] spiral Wraps 3F

8 Mar.- Work on Bridge Bum eats. Gerry over at night lots of Bombs dropping

9 Mar.- Work on Bridge Go to Cafa [café] have eggs and French Fries go to another and have beer peace [sic] of bread and butter for each meal, no grub left.

10 Mar.- Work from 6 A.M. till 9:30 A.M. have Inspec[tion]. Time changes 1hr. Write letters at night.

11 Mar.- Went to Buny get paper and eats work night shift 2 P.M. to 11 P.M.

12 Mar.- Went to Hanu got eats and have good time warm day

13 Mar.- Sleep till noon Work on Bridge Warn Gerry over.

14 Mar.- Sleep late write letters same old work at night eats after

15 Mar.- Sleep late have jam and hard tack in Bed Gerry over at night

16 Mar.- Get up 10 A.M. shave and clean up have Iron rashons [sic]

17 Mar.- Off until In"spec [Inspection] Get Bath go to Irish sparts and at Café in Eve.

18 Mar.- Go to Café at night after working on bridge all day.

19 Mar.- Work on Bridge all day rainy visit ASC[11] at night. Get dates and cheese

---

11 "The officers and men of the [Army Service Corps] were the unsung heroes of the British Army during the Great War. Soldiers can not fight without food, equipment and ammunition. They can not move without horses or vehicles. It was the ASC's job to provide them." ("The Army Service Corps in the First World War," The Long, Long Trail, https://www.longlongtrail.co.uk/army/regiments-and-corps/the-army-service-corps-in-the-first-world-war/, accessed December 8, 2021)

20 Mar.- Work at Canal Bridge Drive start at 10:00 P.M. guns roar constantly

CHAPTER 4

THE GERMAN SPRING OFFENSIVE OF 1918

" The artillery bombardment began at 4:40 a.m. on March 21. The bombardment [hit] targets over an area of 150 square miles, the biggest barrage of the entire war. Over 1,100,000 shells were fired in five hours."[21] This was the largest German offensive since the start of the war. The Germans attacked across a massive front with sixty-two divisions, and the Allied line was in peril of breaking and allowing the Germans to reach Paris.

General Pershing, knowing the gravity of the Allied position, deferred the execution of his plan to form an American army and went to General Foch and said: "I have come to tell you that the American people would consider it a great honor for our troops to be engaged in the present battle. I ask you for this in their name and my own. At this moment there are no other questions but of fighting. Infantry, artillery, aviation, all that we have are yours: use them as you wish. More will come, in numbers equal to requirements. I have come especially to tell you that the American people will be proud to take part in the greatest battle of history."[22]

The Treaty of Brest-Litovsk was a blow to the Allies. The Russians were out of the war. This would allow the Germans to move a large number of troops and equipment to the Western Front. The German High Command believed there may be an opportunity to end the war by using divisions from the Eastern Front to conduct offensive operations and possibly bring the war to a conclusion. They also realized that they needed to conduct this attack before substantial American forces entered the war and shifted the balance of power in men and material to the Allies. General Ludendorff was the mastermind behind the spring offensive, code name "Michael": "His Majesty commands…The Michael attack will take place on March 21. Break into the first hostile position at 9:40 A.M."[23]

The point of attack was the boundary between the British and French armies in the vicinity of Saint-Quentin.

"On March 21, 1918 the first German blow fell on the British along the Somme [River]. After a massive artillery barrage, sixty-two German divisions smashed the British line and achieved a penetration along a fifty mile front. They were heading toward Amiens a communications hub on the Somme that in the German hands would effectively split the French and British armies."[24]

This set up a request from the British for heavy artillery or engineer units from General Pershing. He sent three engineer regiments north.[25]

From papers that my grandfather brought home with him from the war, the 6th Engineers were assigned to the British 1st Cavalry Division.[12] The regiment would earn accolades from the commander of the 1st Cavalry Division for their actions on March 30, 1918.

The Somme Defensive (March 21–April 6, 1918) was the first of five major operations in the Great War in which Howard earned a battle star on his victory ribbon. It was the first of six that he would earn while he was in France (see Appendix 11).

---

12 "The 1st Cavalry Division was one of the first divisions to move to France in 1914, and they would remain on the Western Front throughout the war. It participated in most of the major actions where cavalry were used as a mounted mobile force, and they would also be used as dismounted troops and effectively serve as infantry. On November 11, 1918, orders were received that the division would lead the advance of the British Second Army into Germany. By December 6, having passed through Namur, the division secured the Rhine bridgehead at Cologne. " https://en.wikipedia.org/wiki/1st_Cavalry_Division_(United_Kingdom)

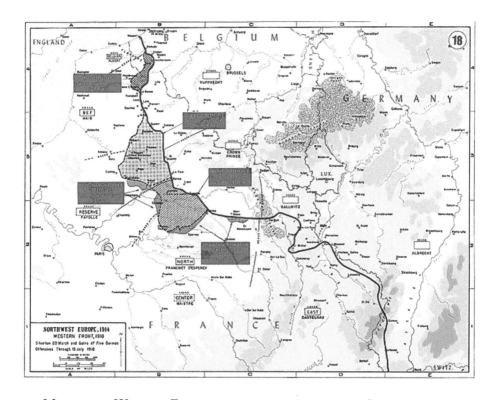

MAP OF THE WESTERN FRONT AND PENETRATION MADE BY GERMAN FORCES DURING THE GERMAN SPRING OFFENSIVE, MARCH 20 TO JULY 18, 1918.

---

21 Mar.- Work at Nesle 12 in shell land all around us people start to move out

22 Mar.- Work on Canal B. Gerry broke through artillery shoot from hill in town Move 11 P.M.

23 Mar.- Out on retreat to Nesle, Manicort join part of Co at Omiecourt hike 20 mi more to Moreuil get in 4 A.M. all in

24 Mar.- Sleeping until 10 A.M. get eats go to Barracks doctor feet[,] fellows come in all day

25 Mar.- Inspection. drill, march about town retire early Gerry over

26 Mar.- Go out and dig Trenches till 11 A.M. Hurry pack up move about 5 mi dig trenches all night

27 Mar.- Dig trenches all day till 4 P.M. pack up go to front on guard all night Sgt. Swingle shot.

—m—

Company B began a retreat, retreating west through Nesle, Omiécourt, and finally to Moreuil. The Germans penetrated the deepest where the 6th Engineers were located, southeast of Amiens. It was in this area where Howard was involved in a frantic move to stop the German advance. Digging trenches for most of the day on March 26 and 27, Howard Claypoole's B Company geared up for a battle with the enemy.

Losses were very heavy at the Somme Defensive in March. Not only had Gough's Fifth Army been sacrificed here, but also some pretty inexperienced Yankee doughboys sacrificed themselves right alongside their beleaguered allies. During this operation, B Company, 6th Engineers suffered 10 killed in action and 28 wounded in action. This was over 14 percent casualties in a company of 264 men during their first action. They fought bravely and held the line.

The British 1st Cavalry Division commander, Major General R. L. Mullen, sent a message to the 6th Engineer regimental commander concerning the support of the engineers during this battle: "I am most grateful to you and the unit under your command for the invaluable assistance you gave us on the 30th March 1918. Please convey my thanks and congratulations to all ranks" (see Appendix 6). It was no small feat to obtain accolades from the British.

The German Spring Offensive continued for a few more months, and while it achieved some tactical success, it was a strategic failure. The Germans failed to split the French and British armies, and they failed to reach their objective at Amiens. More and more American troops would arrive in France. Any chance the Germans had to win the war ended at the Marne.

CHAPTER 5

WOUNDING AND HOSPITALIZATION

The United States entered World War I in April 1917. Over 4.7 million men and women served in the regular US forces, national guard units, and draft units, with about 2.8 million serving overseas. There were 53,402 killed in action, 63,114 deaths from disease and other causes, and about 205,000 wounded.[26]

—⟋⟍—

28 Mar.- Gerry starts. On guard. Battle from noon on get wounded 3 P.M. keep on till 10 P.M. Releaved [*sic*] walk 5 mi to dressing sta.

—⟋⟍—

Howard was wounded in the vicinity of Warfusee-Abancourt, France.

—⟋⟍—

29 Mar.- Go through 3 dressing sta get at Australian sta 4 A.M. leave at 12 noon get to 3rd Canadian[13] 3 P.M. see King.[14] dressed sleep.

—⁓—

The 3rd Canadian General Hospital was a very highly regarded hospital with many members from McGill University.

> During the Great War, McGill University fielded a full general hospital to care for the wounded and sick among the Allied forces fighting in France and Belgium. The unit was designated No. 3 Canadian General Hospital (McGill) and included some of the best medical minds in Canada. Because the unit had a relationship with Sir William Osler, who was a professor at McGill from 1874 to 1885, the unit received special attention throughout the war, and legendary Canadian medical figures such as John McCrae,[15] Edward Archibald, and Francis Scrimger, VC, served on its staff.[27]

—⁓—

---

13 "By the end of the war, No. 3 CGH had admitted 81,689 medical patients and 52,389 wounded; even more astonishing, it had carried out 11,395 operations with a death rate of less than 1%. The unit ceased operations on May 29, 1919, and returned to Canada on July 2 of that year. Most of the unit members would return to Montreal and their hospitals and try to resume their lives and careers." (Andrew Beckett and Edward J. Harvey, "No. 3 Canadian General Hospital (McGill) in the Great War: Service and Sacrifice," *Canadian Journal of Surgery* 61, no. 1 (February 2018): 8–12, https://dx.doi.org/10.1503%2Fcjs.012717)
14 "George V (George Frederick Ernest Albert; June 3, 1865–January 20, 1936) was King of the United Kingdom and the British Dominions, and Emperor of India, from 6 May 1910, until his death in 1936." ("George V," Wikipedia, https://wikipedia.org/wiki/George_V, accessed November 29, 2021)
15 John McCrae was the author of the famous World War I poem "In Flanders Fields."

30 Mar.-leave Can sta 3:30 a.m. ride on train till 1 P.M. land at Hospital Camiers.[16]

31 Mar.- Easter eat sleep and get hair raising shave loose [sic] mustache get little sleep Gerry over

Monday 1 April 1918- Inspection of hospital get good eats. Take exray [sic] of side and shoulder.

—‽—

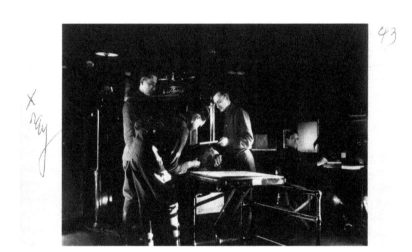

THIS IS A PICTURE OF THE X-RAY MACHINE AT THE HOSPITAL IN CAMIERS.
IT IS HIGHLY LIKELY THAT THIS IS THE EXACT MACHINE THAT HOWARD
CLAYPOOLE WAS X-RAYED WITH ON APRIL 1, 1918. THIS WAS NOT THE FIRST
TIME X-RAYS WERE USED IN A WAR. X-RAYS WERE FIRST USED IN 1897 DURING
THE BALKAN WAR "TO FIND BULLETS AND BROKEN BONES INSIDE PATIENTS."[28]

---

16 "Northwestern's Base Hospital 12, with doctors drawn largely from the university and nurses recruited from the Illinois Training School for Nurses and local hospitals, arrived in Dannes-Camiers, France, in June 1917. Base Hospital 12 was attached to the British Expeditionary Force, taking over the BEF's General Hospital 18 for the duration of the war. For the next 22 months, its medical staff cared for over sixty thousand wounded soldiers, approximately three thousand of whom were American soldiers. Of the six members of the base hospital who died, at least two were Northwestern students." ("Northwestern Remembers the First World War," Northwestern University, *https://sites.northwestern.edu/ww1/hospital*, accessed December 8, 2021)

—w—

2 Apr.- Dull day Australian in to visit rainy Jerry over. Tommie tells stories little sleep

3 Apr.- Rainy operate on side get bullet out don't eat. Little rest

—w—

Howard's wounds were serious. He was struck by two bullets: one in the hip and one in the shoulder. He was first moved to the 3rd Canadian Hospital Camiers, where he first received an X-ray, and then two days later, he was operated on to remove a bullet.

—w—

4 Apr.-Rainy, have victrolas. Tommie dies, eat a little sleep a little

—w—

In the hospital, Howard ran into two friends, Frank Hobbs and Eugene Bostwick. Howard wrote a letter home to his mother dated April 4, 1918: "Bostwick arrived yesterday he was nocked [sic] over three times by shells and blown clear out of the trench once his only injury was a fractured rib. He had trench feaver [sic] after that but seems to be pretty well now."[29]

5 Apr.-Feel better, rainy and cold. Smoke eat and lay in bed Nurse comes in to see us.

6 Apr.- Cold rainy have good eats side bothers at night. Little sleep

7 Apr.- Feel better rain sleep and kid nurses Enjoy life the same old way.

8 Apr.- Inspection have feed at night fried eggs bacon chocolate fruit cigars

9 Apr.- Cloudy, feel fine Another Tommy dies, get buttons.

10 Apr.- Read sleep and eat. Rainy

11 Apr.- Rainy same old stuff still in bed warm in afternoon cool at night

12 Apr.- All is well press feathers all day. Rainy, jokes at night

13 Apr.- Busy day all around Sgt. Hill leaves for front.

14 Apr.- Rainy everything dull Australian entertains at night

15 Apr.- Inspection clean up day, have big eats at night Ausy [*sic*] cook.

16 Apr.- Out of bed for the first walk 3 or 4 yds all in but feel fine.

17 Apr.- Out of bed about 20 minutes have temperature feel good

18 Apr.- W. Myers leaves rain things dull play cards at night in bed

—m—

THESE ARE HOWARD CLAYPOOLE'S PLAYING CARDS THAT HE HAD DURING
THE WAR. RESEARCH CONCERNING THE WALDORF CARD COMPANY
TRACES BACK TO WWI. HE MAY HAVE RECEIVED THESE PLAYING CARDS
AT THE BRITISH HOSPITAL HE WAS IN AFTER HE WAS WOUNDED.

19 Apr.- Myers comes back to see us out of bed play checkers.

20 Apr.- Doctor orders to stay in bed. Cold snow and rain, read and play
cards

21 Apr.- Rain, cold, play chess up again for short time.

22 Apr.- Get up for short time read "Two in the Wilderness".

—◊—

Howard Claypoole's parents received a letter from him on April 22, 1918. This letter made it into the local newspaper back home in New Jersey.

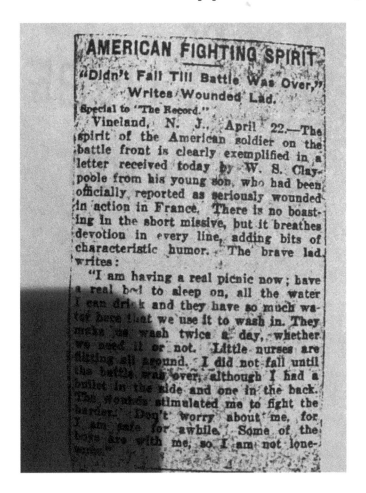

> **VINELAND BOY WOUNDED**
>
> Howard Claypoole, Injured in Big Bat-
> tle in France
>
> Vineland, N. J., April 8 (Special).—A
> telegram to Mr. and Mrs. W. S. Clay-
> poole, today notifies them their son
> Howard Claypoole was seriously wound-
> ed in battle in France, March 28.
> Young Claypoole enlisted October 8 in
> the Sixth Engineering Corps. He left
> December 4 for "over there."

TWO NEWSPAPER ARTICLES THAT ANNOUNCE HOWARD CLAYPOOLE
WAS WOUNDED IN FRANCE (UNKNOWN NEWSPAPERS).

The smaller article reads:

VINELAND BOY WOUNDED
Howard Claypoole Injured in Big Battle in France
Vineland, N.J., April 8 (Special). A telegram to Mr. and Mrs. W. S. Claypoole, today notifies them their son Howard Claypoole was seriously wounded in battle in France, March 28. Young Claypoole enlisted October 8 in the Sixth Engineering Corps. He left December 4 for "Over There."

—⚍—

23 Apr.- Read and lay around go out side [*sic*] for a few minutes

24 Apr.- Clean shoes shine Miss Simmons shoes

25 Apr.- Read, play chess and cards Miss Simmons leaves

26 Apr.- Play chess rain take little walk. Get hair cut read.

27 Apr.-McPherson and Mess Sgt. go back to Co. Rec'd reg letter Bye [*sic*] chocolate

28 Apr.- Things slow cloudy day play chess tell Army tales

29 Apr.- Inspection sailor from J.City comes in to visit

30 Apr.- Same old thing Rain cold and play chess

Wednesday 1 May 1918- Nice day feel bum in bed early

2 May- Rain still bad play chess and get little sleep

3 May- Rain in morning clear rest of day play chess

4 May- Miss Morrissey makes cake play chess nice day

—⟋⟍—

I was able to find out a little bit of information about Nurse May Morrissey. She was born in Will County, Illinois, went to school in Will County, and was the first nurse to serve in World War I from Will County. She also married in Joliet, and her married name was Mrs. Harold M. Coon. She was a student nurse from 1913 to 1916 before she volunteered to go to France.

—⟋⟍—

5 May- Rain like the devil lay in bed all morning

6 May- Inspection every thing fine feel a little better

7 May- Draw clothes to leave for R.G. #2 some day

—⟋⟍⟍—

For over a month after the first operation, Howard recovered from his wounds, but something was not right, and he had to go to another hospital for another procedure.

—⟋⟍⟍—

8 May- Leave 18th Gen 8 A.M. Arr. Paris 10:30 P.M. Arr #2 2 A.M. Some Ride

—⟋⟍⟍—

On May 8, he traveled to Paris and then on to Base Hospital 34 in Nantes. He appears to have been moved to this hospital because further surgery on his hip was necessary.

—⟋⟍⟍—

9 May- Lay around all day + rest up look over Hosp. Lights out at 9 P.M.

10 May- Get clothes go out on Boulivard [sic] see many chickins [sic] out again at night

11 May- Leave at 8 A.M. arr at Base Hosp #34 Nants[17] 4:30 P.M. see more of the fellows have good eats

---

17 "Meanwhile, to the few officers and men remaining came orders to proceed to Nantes— another Loire Valley city—the point that had been decided upon as the final home of Base Hospital 34. Ahead of them lay the problem of preparing what buildings had been chosen for the hospital itself. A French seminary was to be used as the central hospital. Before supplies could be utilized, it was necessary to remodel the seminary itself. There were barracks to be built, roads to be resurfaced, warehouses to be cleared—all to be finished before actual hospitalization of wounded could be realized. With the completion of such preparations came word that the unit was again to be reunited. Detachments that had been absent for months began to return. On April 1st, the hospital was ready—word was sent to headquarters—and in the following months its actual work of caring for thousands of wounded

12 May- Sleep most of day bunk next to W.P.Allen very tired

13 May- Part of bone cut out all in hurt like the devil. Sleep.

—⚒—

14 May- Exray [*sic*] taken so see eye Dr. He gives me cigarette good fellow

15 May- Shave clean up play cards Rain.

16 May- Get clothes nice day sit out under trees enjoy real life play cards at night

17 May- Write letters in morning sit out in grove in afternoon

18 May- Hobbs comes in have good old talk out in grove Some Life.

19 May- Play cards out in grove talk and sleep

20 May–25 May- Nothing happen tiresome as hell eat, sleep, sit in shade Headake [*sic*] Spanish Feaver [*sic*] Disgusted!

26 May- Feel bum go to church

27 May- Feel <u>Rotten</u>

28–29 May- Lay around

30 May- [no entry]

31 May- Feel better

---

soldiers was being accomplished daily. (Edmund M. Pitts, ed., *Base Hospital 34 in the World War* (Philadelphia: Lyon & Armor, 1922), 14–15", https://collections.nlm.nih.gov/catalog/nlm:nlmuid-14230650R-bk)

1 June 1918, Saturday- go out in grove OK again

2 June- Go to services nice day press grass

3 June- "   " Either no entry or he did the same thing from 2 June

4 June- Leave bandage off for first time side feels good

5 June- Work on chow wagon Some job.

6 June- Quite chow wagon at night. Can't get pass so strike.

7 June- Watch the birds fly + leaves rustle while Parker tells stories

8 June- All is well nice day every one in good spirit.

9 June- Go to open air service. Nice day

10 June- Get letter from DK with Dollar in it write back.

11 June- Bostwick gets Package eat candy Oh Boy.

—⚬⚬⚬—

Finally, after two operations, Howard seems fit for duty—three months after he was wounded, which, I believe, speaks to the seriousness of his wounds. His diary does not in any way relay the pain and suffering he was going through after surgeries. But the length of time to recover from these surgeries speaks volumes as to how seriously he was wounded. Howard wound up in the 18th General Hospital Camiers.

From March 30 to June 12, he recuperated in hospitals. He was wounded in the shoulder and in the side. It was necessary to remove part of the bone in his hip. I don't believe he was as well as he led one to believe from his diary and his letters home. The food he received during his hospitalization appeared to be better than average. Numerous inspections were held during his stay in the hospital. Howard endured his hospitalization by playing chess, reading, writing letters, telling war stories, and playing cards.

—∿—

12 June- Leave Base #34 9:30 P.M. reach Angers 12:30 A.M.

13 June- Leave Angers 4 A.M. arr[ive] Tours 8:30 A.M. Leave 11:30 A.M. reach St Aignon Noyers 4:30 P.M.

14 June- Bostwick + Small arr. Go to town at night

15 June- Not much doing sleep and eat wait for orders

16 June- called out in morning go to train 10:30 A.M. Leave 4:30 P.M.

17 June- Arr Is- sur-tille 4:30 p.m. go to rest camp go to Y.M. with Al Compton

18 June- Leave at 6:30 and arr about 11:30 at Laignes

19 June- On guard all day + night sick.

20 June- Feel Bum lay around all day Rain + muddy

21 June- Go to Dr. marked quarters rain most of day.

22 June- Feel better draw equipment. Rain a little Sleeping with one blanket on board floor

23 June- Move to Billitts [billets] with cement floor. All day off.

24 June- On detale [*sic*] in morning. Skip it go out in Park all day

25 June- Skip to Park all day, leave at 6:30 P.M. ride all night

26 June- Arr at Bains Les Bains 8:30 A.M. Bum Chow

27 June- Stay in Billets most all day Look over the town at night.

28 June- Hang around all day take walk at night. Nice weather.

29 June- Drill in morning Off in afternoon visit girls at night.

—ᘏᘏ—

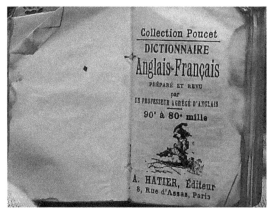

This is the English-French dictionary that Howard carried during the war. This little dictionary measured about two inches by one inch.

—༄—

30 June- Pick strawberries and cherries with Mime, visit Mlle at night. Gray Com rape.

Monday, 1 July 1918- work about half hour off rest of day. Visit M'lle at night

2 July- Drill in morning off all afternoon go for swim visit M'lle

3 July- Leave Bains Les Bains 6:30 arr, Chatigney [*sic*] 11 P.M. stay all night

4 July- Leave at 5:30 A.M. Ride all day rain in morning arr. La Bourget 2 A.M.

5 July- Leave 10 A.M. arr Noisy Le Sec 11 A.M. Leave 3 P.M. arr Bossy 8:30 P.M. sleep in wagons

—༄—

On June 12, the party was over as Howard started his journey back to the 3rd Division. He traveled through Angers, Tours, Saint-Aignan, Noyers, Is-sur-Tille, Laignes, Bains-les-Bains, Châtigny, Le Bourget, Noisy-le-Sec, and Bossy.

—༄—

6 July- Leave for 3rd DIV arr Hdg & PM. Sleep in carpanter [*sic*] shop have great feed.

—༄—

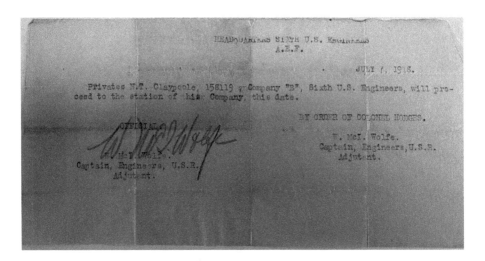

PRIVATE CLAYPOOLE RECEIVED AN ORDER ON JULY 7 FROM HEADQUARTERS 6TH ENGINEERS, AEF: "WILL PROCEED TO THE STATION OF HIS COMPANY, THIS DATE."

Howard Claypoole was back at the front for no more than a week when the Germans tried one last attempt to possibly bring the war to a conclusion on their terms. B Company would again go into combat.

CHAPTER 6

THE CHAMPAGNE-MARNE DEFENSIVE

The Aisne-Marne Offensive

A t this point of the war, the Germans had little chance of winning the war. The United States' entry in the war with hundreds of thousands of troops had clearly tipped the balance of power to the Allies. The Germans, however, thought a last attack may allow them to go to the peace table on somewhat favorable terms.

> The first German boat waves began crossing the Marne just before 2 A.M. Riding twenty to the boat, the attackers got in just under the embankment and waited. The night was ink black. From the other side, pioneers brought forward footbridges on which men could cross single file. Engineers came with pontoons, and behind them were horses, guns, and motor vehicles jamming toward the crossing. The whole [German] Seventh Army was in motion.[30]

—ɯɯ—

7 July- Leave for Co. about 10 A.M. hike eat with 30th take Bath Arr. 8. P.M. Great Welcome

—⚏—

He arrived back at his unit on July 7, 1918, and received a nice homecoming: "I arrived in camp about 8 P.M. last Sunday the 7th and rec'd a royal reception most of the fellows are most naked in a cootie hunt. Chas and I have just finished killing a few off now but this is the life I am sure glad to be back with the boys."[31]

—⚏—

8 July- Have morning off dig trenches in afternoon gas + shelling at night move

—⚏—

PHOTO OF HOWARD CLAYPOOLE IN FRANCE CIRCA 1918
(PHOTO COURTESY OF JEFFREY CLAYPOOLE).

Gas. Probably one of the most frightening weapons ever used in warfare. The Germans first used gas in 1915. The first gas used was chlorine, but later on, the Germans began using mustard gas. It is highly likely that mustard gas is what was falling around the engineers.

—◊—

9 July- Dig trenches all day on guard at night shelling at night

10 July- On guard all day heavy barrage at night

11 July- Trim brush in morning off in afternoon rain at night

12 July- String B[arbed] wire and out line [*sic*] trenches rain most of day

13 July- Work all day Jerry shells at night. Wind up.

14 July- Off all day clean up Jerry starts Barrage 11 P.M. till Morn.

—◊—

During early July, the Germans, under the command of General Ludendorff, were concerned about whether they should attack or go on the defensive. That they did not go on the defensive is surprising considering the arrival of multiple US divisions in France: "As Ludendorff put it: '…not only had our March superiority in the number of divisions been cancelled, but even the difference gross numbers was now to our disadvantage, for an American division consists of twelve strong battalions.'"[32]

On July 15, the Germans launched their last major offensive of the war. The goal of this attack was to once more try and get the Allies to come to the table and end the war. The Germans called this offensive "the Friedensturm, or peace offensive—its object to widen the salient begun in the May offensive, and to continue the advance on Paris. The shells rained on the US Third Division's positions on the Marne for three hours."[33]

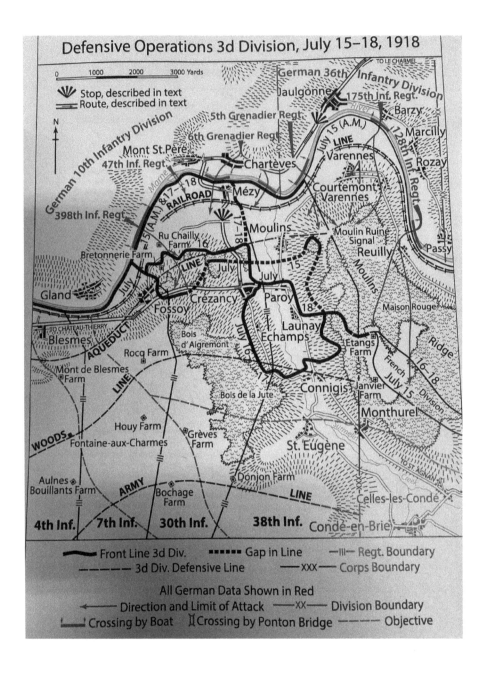

Defensive Operations 3d Division, July 15–18, 1918

The 3rd Division owned a seven-mile front along the Marne River. Defensively, the position had some weaknesses where its boundary linked up with a French division on the southern boundary. The terrain favored the Germans in several areas: "The north boundary of the 3rd Division sector was formed by the canalized Marne, there about fifty yards wide and fifteen feet deep. The hills on the enemy side of this sharply cleft valley are heavily wooded and rise to 450 feet."[34]

The battle on the fifteenth involved the 38th Infantry Regiment. This regiment, commanded by Colonel McAlexander, would earn accolades for the defense the regiment executed at the Marne. This is where the 3rd Division picked up the nickname "Rock of the Marne."

—⚓—

15 July- Jerry shells all day 5 hurt Move up to res[erve]. At night

—⚓—

Fortunately, the Germans were stopped at the Marne, and the engineers of B Company were not thrown in to the breach to stop the German attack. Unlike during the Somme Defensive, the engineers were not required to fill in as infantrymen. And "by nightfall [July 15] the enemy attack across the Marne was completely defeated in the 3rd Division sector."[35]

—⚓—

16 July- In Dugouts all day Jerry shells 5 or 6 casuals [casualties] Move closer.

17 July- Chas wounded move back to old camp Rain.

18 July- On out post all day shelled at night dig trenches.

—⚓—

The period of July 15–18, 1918, was considered a major operation called the Champagne-Marne Defensive. This is the operation where Howard earned his second battle star on his victory ribbon. He was not in direct combat with German forces, but in his diary, he says that men were wounded three of the four days due to German artillery fire.

On the eighteenth, the Allies launched an attack of their own. This attack involved five American divisions. The 3rd Division was attached to the French Ninth Army. The Franco-American attack came as a tactical and operational surprise to the Germans. [36]

—〰—

19 July- Get shelled dig trenches at night lots of gas[18]

20 July- Get shelled out at night several gasses Silkie killed, Rain Joe + I sleep together

21 July- Move to Mezy get shelled out on patrol steve + other wounded

—〰—

Here Howard Claypoole's diary is a little vague about his actual performance on the twenty-first. *The History of the Sixth Engineers* specifically mentions Private Claypoole: "Everyone breathed a momentary sigh of relief when he [Private Stevens] was ferried safely across, but Private Claypoole, who did the ferrying, went back and forth many times."[37]

---

18 "On April 22, 1915 at 5 p.m., a wave of asphyxiating gas released from cylinders embedded in the ground by German specialist troops smothered the Allied line on the northern end of the Ypres Salient, causing panic and a struggle to survive a new form of weapon. The attack forced two colonial French divisions north of Ypres from their positions, creating a 5-mile gap in the Allied line defending the city. This was the first effective use of poison gas on the Western Front and the debut of Germany's newest weapon in its chemical arsenal, chlorine gas, which irritated the lung tissue causing a choking effect that could cause death." ("First Use of Poison Gas," The National WWI Museum and Memorial, https://www.theworldwar. org/support/donate-object/recentacquisition/poison-gas, accessed December 8, 2021)

—w—

22 July- Move up river get shelled put in bridge Move back to Mezy

23 July- Work on bridge all day + all night get shelled.

—w—

The diaries do not do these couple of days justice. B Company was able to put in a bridge in the vicinity of Fossoy. This bridge was built while under artillery and sniper fire. The engineers worked through the night to build the bridge at Mézy-sur-Seine: "Eight A.M. of the morning of the 23rd saw the work complete after a night of pouring rain and continual shelling, and the first vehicle, a ration wagon, passed over."[38]

—w—

24 July- Move past Jourgonne 4th platoon get shelled Bommed [*sic*] + sniped at.

25 July- Stay in Cave all day get shelled have good sleep + rest. pretty safe.

—w—

The History of the Sixth Engineers mentions this cave:

> On the 24th First Lieutenant J. J. Cronin was sent with a detachment of thirty-five men to work on the roads in the vicinity of Le Charmel. This detachment found a wonderful dugout in the shape of an old chalk mine about two kilometers from the town of Le Charmel. Long disuse had caused the mine to become almost filled with water, but the platoon found room enough for quarters and dwelt safe from enemy shells or bombs.[39]

3d Div
France, 25 July'18, 18 h 30

ORDERS
No. 156
1-3.

1. The following signals are prescribed for use by the Infantry:

Objective reached".................................... 6 white stars
"Request for barrage fire".......................... 1 red fire
Friendly Field Artillery is firing upon us".......... Caterpillar
Friendly Heavy Artillery is firing upon us........... Caterpillar, followed by
one green fire.
We are progressing; lengthen the fire .... 5 white stars
Ammunition .... 1 white fire followed by o
green fire.

2. Signals between aeroplane and Infantry remain unchanged.

3. Upon receiving the signal "Where are you" from an aeroplane, the front li
will be lined out by means of individual panels.

All troops must be constantly on the watch for this signal.

ROBERT H.C. KELTON,
Colonel, General Staff,
Chief of Staff.

ORDER SAVED BY HOWARD CLAYPOOLE DESCRIBING
SIGNALS IN EFFECT ON JULY 25, 1918.

—〰—

26 July- Lay low all day Beaucoup shelling Lay with 30th Inf. All night in rain shelled

27 July- Go out in afternoon Joe comes up with 5 other bunch work at night

—〰—

The 3rd Division and the 6th Engineers had participated in heavy fighting vicinity of the Marne River for roughly a month. They had both served in the defense of the Marne and then crossed it and gone on the offensive. The unit was about to get relieved for their efforts.

> To the East of Château Thierry, the AEF troops also played a significant role. The 3rd Division had been a mainstay of the Marne line since early June. Initially, its role was to pin down the German forces as the Sixth and Tenth Armies advanced. After July 20, as part of the French XXXVIII Corps the Division crossed the Marne, cleared the Northern bank, and pursued the Germans as they withdrew. The division pushed forward until relieved by the 32nd Division on July 29.[40]

This concluded the major engagement called the Aisne-Marne Offensive. The dates on his order differ from the 3rd Division military history. His military history lists the Aisne-Marne Offensive from July 18–27, 1918, while his order, dated July 7, 1919, lists the dates as July 18 and August 6, 1918. Howard earned his third battle star to his victory ribbon during this operation.

—⚬—

28 July- Work all day nice day a little shelling lots of troops come up

29 July- Work all day fine day move back to Chartouse bombed at night

30 July- Work in morn put up tent lay around in afternoon

31 July- Move to H.Q. lay around all day

—⚬—

In July, they suffered three gas attacks that resulted in at least one killed in action. The Germans at this point of the war were predominantly using mustard gas, which blistered the skin, eyes, and lungs. The use of gas by the Germans must be considered an effective weapon: "Gas inflicted over a quarter of all AEF casualties, one of each U. S. Division's four field hospitals had to be dedicated to treatment of gas injuries."[41] Shelling also caused significant casualties. The diary notes that during July, thirteen to fourteen members of B Company were wounded by artillery fire.

Much of July was spent digging trenches, trimming brush, stringing barbed wire, outlining trenches, and building bridges. Howard mentions lots of shelling and use of gas during July; casualties mentioned were approximately fifteen wounded and one killed. Operations of the 3rd Division included the Champagne-Marne Defensive, and the Aisne-Marne Offensive. The 3rd Division was located on the Marne.

The southern boundary was ridges further back from the river and farmland that was sparsely forested. There were several areas that were possible rallying points for the attacking German forces that posed a threat to all the defensive positions set up on the south bank of the Marne.

—m—

Thursday, 1 Aug. 1918- On K.P. all day Chas comes back move up on hill.

2 Aug.- Go on sick call get 2 teeth filled rained all day. Moved at night

3 Aug.-Work on bridge all day near Gouancourt [sic] both bridges work all night rain hard

4 Aug.- Work all day sleep in billitts [sic] at night get champayne [sic]

5 Aug.- Finish Bridge fix road to Colonyes start another bridge

6 Aug.- Work on bridge a Gerry dump go back Co. at Argy Le Ponsart [Arcis-le-Ponsart]

7 Aug.- Fix bridge at Courville get shelled sleep well.

8 Aug.- Fourth Pla[toon]. Stay in others work at Courville 9 wounded 3 killed shelled.

9 Aug.- Go out in afternoon close to line get shelled return two balloons shot down

10 Aug.- Go out to fix road get shelled return start back for H.Q. hike about 12 kilo about mid nt.[midnight]

—⚊—

Between August 3 and August 10, B Company was building or repairing five bridges and several roads. While they repaired these bridges and roads, they were often shelled and suffered casualties. Oftentimes they were very close to the front doing repairs.

—⚊—

11 Aug.- Lay around in morning get trucks in afternoon go back to H.Q. at Fassoy

12 Aug.- Lay around get clothes write letters Go for swim +boat ride at night

13 Aug.- Lay around all day cook spuds + toast bread at night Orders to leave

14 Aug.- Leave Foosoy [sic] hike 20 mi to Mont mirail [sic] very much in

15 Aug.- On K.P. Leave camp 3:30 load on train + leave about 6:30 P.M.

16 Aug.- Arrive at Lemange- Aux – Eux [Demange-aux-Eux] 6 A.M. See Buckie leave 10:30 A.M. Arr. Couvertpeuits 3 P.M.

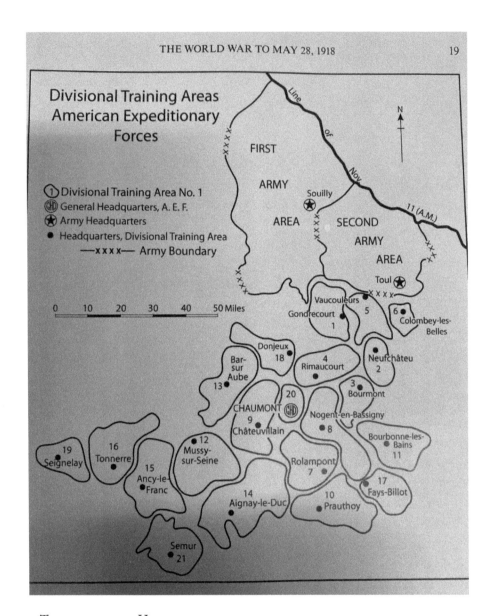

THE AREA WHERE HOWARD CONDUCTED TRAINING IS PICTURED ON THE ABOVE
MAP. GONDRECOURT, LISTED AS NUMBER 1 ON THE MAP, IS WHERE THE 6TH
ENGINEERS CONDUCTED TRAINING FROM AUGUST 16 TO SEPTEMBER 4, 1918.

17 Aug.- Clean up street + roam around town some town!

18 Aug.- Clean streets go for a bath in afternoon 3 platoon comes in.

19 Aug.- Drill in morning move 2 P.M. to Montiers with H.Q. Some Y.M.C.A. kid

20 Aug.- Drill in morning on range in afternoon. Get payed [*sic*] 500 F 17 champaign [*sic*] at night.

21 Aug.- Drill all day Banquet tired at night

22 Aug.- Drill all day hot as hell Col. Took us over Beer at night

23 Aug.- Drill in Morn scrimish [*sic*] drill in afternoon sign payroll at night

24 Aug.- passing Review + Inspection all afternoon off. Beer at night. Notes_ Montiers – Sur- Saulx

25 Aug.- Off all day go to see Mlle Guard at night rain a little

26 Aug.- Drill all day scool [*sic*] in afternoon Visit at night Some time in!

27 Aug.- Drill and have school Same in afternoon

28 Aug.- Drill all day see Mlle at night

29 Aug.- Go on sick call off all day write letter

30 Aug.- Marked duty go out in afternoon see Mlle + have wine + beer.

31 Aug.- Inspection in morning rest of day off

Sunday 1 September, 1918- Go to Ballgame with girls, visit in afternoon have beer + wine.

2 Sep.- Col's orderly releaved [*sic*] 10:30 P.M. some day drilled in morning

3 Sep.- Col orderly in morning afternoon off

— ɯ —

From August 16 to September 4, 1918, Howard was in the vicinity of Gondrecourt, France. According to the military history for Howard Claypoole, this time period is listed as "Training Period Gondrecourt Area." The diary lists drilling on nine different days and some range time for marksmanship training. There also appears to be a significant amount of free time for the soldiers of B Company as they had quite a few evenings free. Howard mentions going to see mademoiselles three times and then also mentions going to a baseball game with girls.

— ɯ —

4 Sep.- Leave Montiers 8:30 PM fall out of hike at Mandres

[This is the only hike that Howard mentions that he fell out of during his time with B Company. It appears that the wound to his hip suffered in March caused him pain during extended road marches.]

5 Sep.- Wake up 7:30 A.M. get wine eggs + cheese reach Co. about 3:30 P.M. Leave again 8:30

6 Sep.- Arrive at Deluce lay around + clean up all day rain in afternoon

7 Sep.- Inspection at 8:30 A.M. off rest of day Baseball game H.Q. + A Co

8 Sep.- Football game B+C Co. Co. C wins rain at night have good rest

—〜—

Keeping the troops occupied and busy is always a method for commanders to keep the troops from getting into trouble. Sports have always been a big part of the army, and even though there is a lot of drilling, schooling, and skirmishing going on to prepare for future combat, there is time for sports. On September 7, there was a baseball game between Headquarters Company and A Company, and on September 8, there was a football game between B and C Companies, which C Company had the honor of winning.

—〜—

9 Sep.- Drill all morning rain hard drill in afternoon leave late at night rain

10 Sep.- Camp in woods side of hill rain all wet. Leave again at night

11 Sep.- Arrive in woods camp rain still wet leave at night

12 Sep.- Arrive close to line in early morning rain move on at night

13 Sep.- Arr. In woods rain look over tanks + trenches move to Easey

14 Sep.- Off in morning get shelled work on roads to Maigeiris all shot up pack + leave at 9 P.M. hike until 8 A.M. next morning

—〜—

This was the lull before the storm. The next day, the company was on the move toward the front. The men moved at night and camped during the day in the woods. This movement continued for five days. On September 14, the company worked on roads to Margarais; they moved out on the same day at 9:00 p.m. and hiked until the next morning.

The Saint-Mihiel Offensive occurred during the dates September 12–16, 1918. Howard's participation was only September 12–14, but he was awarded his fourth battle star for participation in this operation. He and his unit survived this operation with only some shelling.

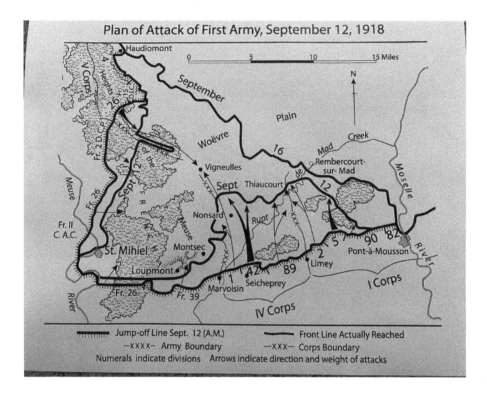

Plan of Attack of First Army, September 12, 1918

—ຫ—

15 Sep.- Camp in woods between Boucq + Connieville stay in all day kitchen leaves sleep

16 Sep.- Get up 10 A.M. cook bacon fry bread, coffee, same for dinner catch cold!! Rain

17 Sep.- Fry bacon spuds + bread go for swim leave 3:30 P.M.

18 Sep.- Ride in trucks until 5 A.M. go past Eppicourt sleep with arabs leave 10:30 A.M.

19 Sep.- In woods by Julecourt rain + cold cook bacon coffee + bread

20 Sep.- Kitchen arrives gas mask inspection Houghton, Benny and I pitch tent together

—⁓—

On September 20, 1918, Howard Claypoole received a promotion. In a letter dated September 30, 1918, he states, "I was made Pvt. 1st Class Sept 20 ($3.00 more a mo.) and entered the office Sept. 25 as Mail Orderly and Clerk." According to Howard's paybook, he made $36.60 a month as a private first class.[42] When Howard was promoted to corporal, his paycheck went up to $40.80, and at the time he was discharged at the end of the war, his pay had been hiked up to $42.80 per month.

As mail orderly, Howard had a cushy job sorting mail behind the lines. His quarters were a little more comfortable than the pup tents he had been camping in with his fellow engineers. Company clerk is usually located with the commander and the senior non-commissioned officer, as he handles all the required paperwork in the company. He is no longer on the front lines building bridges, digging trenches, or serving as infantry under certain circumstances.

—⁓—

21 Sep.- Drill in morning Rain Engr. Drill in afternoon rain at night Notes- Made 1st class Sept. 20.

22 Sep.- Drill in morning get payed [sic] at noon rain in afternoon + night move

23 Sep.- Arrive nearer line about 4 A.M. camp on side of hill rainy + wet sleep

24 Sep.- Cut trails thro' woods all day little barrage at night

25 Sep.- Look over trail in morning to on office work – Betaglainville-

26 Sep.- Work in office beaucoup mail Co moves 7 A.M. about 6 kilo Stay back with Sgt. Brundage rain

27 Sep.- Rain mail in get one letter from Jo. Busy with old mail.

28 Sep.- Rain a little same work busy until late at night good eats

29 Sep.- Work all day in office hear of fellow 9 in all being hurt by cap of shell. Rain.

30 Sep.- Move to new dugout get stove and all comforts some life

Tuesday, 1 October 1918- Brundage sick leaves for Candidate school at night rain

2 Oct.- Run things alone some day soft going

3 Oct.- Capt. Sgt. Breneman + Allen come in + look things over Breneman takes charge

4 Oct.- Allen comes in straightens things out Jerry over at night feel bum

5 Oct.- Feel bum sleep until 8 A.M. breakfast pretty soft

—w—

This is the last entry in the smaller diary Howard kept during the war. Maintaining the diary was quite the accomplishment, to make entries day in and day out under trying conditions. The diary provides a glimpse into his character and his obvious enjoyment of good food as that is something he seems to always comment on in his diary. The period of his recovery from being shot is a glimpse into the hospitals in World War I.

In a letter dated October 11, 1918, Howard makes some insights into casualties his unit suffered:

> And you can look at the pictures taken at the barracks and say that Howard is the only one still with + representing the Reg.-Hobbs in the States. Joe has been in the Hosp since about Aug. 1st. all the rest left about the time I did and haven't come back, Bostwick still in the hospital and several more of my old pals there-so that's the way things go. We had eight more casualties today. But yours truly has a swell job now and just stay close enough to get the reports. Oh this is some life. I almost feel ashamed to keep this job, but I guess I almost deserve it.[43]

CHAPTER 7
MEUSE-ARGONNE OFFENSIVE

The Meuse Argonne Offensive was the last great offensive of the war. A significant part of the offensive was the American Expeditionary Force that had grown from just a few divisions into a large army of fifteen divisions for this offensive.

> "Over 820,000 men were transferred in the [Meuse-Argonne] region; 220,000 French and Italian troops left the area, and about 600,000 Americans entered. Of the 15 American Divisions that took over the sector, 7 had been involved in the St. Mihiel operation, 3 came from the Vesle sector, 3 from the area of Soissons ,1 near Bar-Duc sector, and 1 from a training area.
>
> The AEF's attack into the Meuse Argonne region was part of [Marshall] Foch's general offensive against the Germans...For this grand offensive, Foch had 220 divisions, of which forty-two were the big divisions of the AEF.[44]

The gap between the small diary and the large diary is very significant and cannot be explained. One explanation is that he could not write any more until he received a new diary, but this is just speculation. The large diary starts out with the famous words "Over the top" on October 20. "Over the top" is the phrase used during the war when a unit left its trenches to attack. Attacks against machine guns, mortars, and artillery usually led to a large number of casualties.

—⚏—

20 Oct.- Over the top 7 am carry on. Capt. Harris wounded, captured + died in German Field Hosp. Lt. Elsworth killed 5 P.M. Cpl. Heal Bowrassa, Kummer Pvt. Henry, Herrera, Olien, Magness killed. Houghton Ward, Canonico, Turco, Duhrkoop + O'hara taken prisoners

—⚏—

The History of the Sixth Engineers provides more detail on what happened to Captain Harris during the attack on October 20 in the midmorning:

> Shortly afterward Captain Harris, while wrestling a machine gun from an enemy posse and turning it upon them, received a bullet in his lungs and another in the leg. At 1 P.M. barely breathing, he was placed on a stretcher to be carried to the rear. Captain Knerr then assumed command of Company B.[45]

A litter party attempted to carry Captain Harris to the rear and was captured by the Germans. This explains how he ended up dying in a German field hospital.

—⚏—

24 Oct.- Cpl Allen killed

28 Oct.- Releaved [*sic*] from front line 4 A.M. hike back to camp two kilo Sou of Montfaucon

—⚏—

B Company suffered massive casualties during this offensive at the Meuse-Argonne. The 6th Engineer history lists the following casualties during the period September 27, 1918, to October 25, 1918: fifteen killed in action (KIA), twenty-five wounded in action (WIA), and one engineer listed as a prisoner of war (POW). These are significant losses for any unit, and it is understandable that they were pulled out of the line. Note that B Company was a company of engineers, yet they could fight as infantrymen in any given situation. During this action, they fought as infantrymen, attacked like infantrymen, and defended ground like infantrymen. It is a credit to the unit training, leadership, and American fighting spirit of all the engineers that they fought so valiantly and achieved a hard-won victory on the battlefield. The attack of October 20 kept the men on the front line for eight days, after which they were relieved from the front line and were allowed the well-deserved liberty of a bath and some clean clothes.

This was the fifth battle star earned by Howard Claypoole in the Great War.

—⁂—

29 Oct.- Baths + clothing issue

30 Oct.- Repair Nantillios-Septsarges Road Prepair [*sic*] to move at 8:30 P.M.

31 Oct.- Leave camp 2 A.M. hike to camp in wood three kilo north of Recicourt arr 7 AM

First of November, 1918- Leave camp 9:30 AM hike to R'court load on trucks leave at 12:30 P.M. for Nancois-La-petite Arr 6:00 P.M.

2 Nov–10 Nov.- Co. duties

9 Nov.- Rec'd Replacements 49

—∿—

The company was soon after on the move, repairing a road near Nantillois and then moving to a wood near Récicourt. On November 1, they loaded up on trucks and moved to Nancois Le-Petite. Howard was stuck with company duties November 2–10. On November 9, he notes that the company has received forty-nine replacements, an indication of how heavy B Company's casualties had been up to this point in time.

—∿—

10 Nov.- Orders to leave for front

CHAPTER 8

THE WAR ENDS AND OCCUPATION DUTY

General Orders

No 203   FRANCE,
November 12. 1918

The enemy has capitulated. It is fitting that I address myself in thanks directly to the officers and soldiers of the American Expeditionary Forces who by their heroic efforts have made possible this glorious result. Our armies, hurriedly raised and hastily trained, met a veteran enemy, and by courage, discipline and skill always defeated him. Without complaint you have endured incessant toil, privation and danger. You have seen many of your comrades make the supreme sacrifice that freedom may live. I thank you for the patience and courage with which you have endured. I congratulate you upon the splendid fruits of victory which your heroism and the blood of our gallant dead are now presenting to our nation. Your deeds will live forever on the most glorious pages of American history.

[signed] John J Pershing
General, Commander in Chief
American Expeditionary Forces

—∿∿—

11 Nov.- Ready to leave 8:30 AM Armistice declared order changed resume drill

—∿∿—

Howard's lack of exuberance of the end of the war is clear in his diary. No exclamation points, no "THE WAR IS OVER!!!!" in capital letters and his emotionless reaction is echoed in *The History of the Sixth Engineers*:

> The news [of the Armistice] aroused no particular exuberant feelings among the troops. They were pleased, of course, but rather listless. Five weeks of high nervous tension had deadened their capacity for spontaneous outbursts. They wanted just one thing—to go home where they could forget.[46]

Bravo Company, 6th Engineers, after serving in every major engagement, suffered 33 KIA and 82 WIA out of a 264-man company, almost 50 percent casualties. The use of the engineers as infantrymen contributed significantly to these losses. The Saint-Mihiel Offensive resulted in the most casualties of the war for the company (15 KIA and 25 WIA), including the company commander.

—∿∿—

12 Nov.–14 Nov.- Drill Co. Duties

14 Nov.- Leave Nancois 11:00 AM load on trucks on Bar-le-duc road leave 11:30 AM for Veviville arr 8:00 P.M.

15 Nov.- Lay around + cook own grub cabbage + green tomatoes in water

16 Nov.- Leave V. 7:30 P.M. hike to Woel sleep out in field

17 Nov.- leave W. 5:30 AM hike to Conflans arr 2:30 P.M.

18 Nov.- Leave C. 7 AM hike to Brie arr 11:30 AM

19 Nov.- Co. Duties

20 Nov.- Leave B. 8:30 AM Cross line into Lorraine at 10:40 AM arr at Nilvingen 1:20 P.M.

21 Nov.- Leave N- 1:00 P.M. hike to Diedenhofen arr 4 P.M.

22 Nov.- Leave D- 12 noon hike to Kechingen arr 2:30 P.M.

23 Nov.- Leave K- 7:30 AM hike to Euringen arr. 11:30

24 Nov.-

25 Nov.- medals awards

26 Nov.–30 Nov.- Co Duties Thanksgiving (Chicken dinner)

1 Dec.- Leave E- 8:30 AM cross Luxenburgh [sic] into Germany 11:30 PM arr at Kirf 3:00 A.M. Dec. 2nd

3 Dec.- Leave K- 8 AM hike to Hentern arr 4:30 P.M.

4 Dec.- Leave H- 9-A.M. to Reinsfeld arr 3:30 P.M.

5 Dec.- Leave R- 8:30 AM hike to camp in woods rain arr 6 P.M.

6 Dec.- Leave camp 8:00 AM hike to Hottenbach arr 4:30 P.M.

7 Dec.- Leave H. 7 A.M. hike to Schmiedel arr 8:40 P.M.

8 Dec.- Co Duties

9 Dec.- Leave S- 12:30 P.M. hike to Argenthal arr 3:30 PM

10 Dec.- Leave A- 9:00 AM hike to Bacharach on Rhine arr 5-P.M.

11 Dec.-

—⁓—

In a letter dated December 11, 1918, Howard mentions how many men are left in the Company: "There are 81 in the Co now that came over with us out of 264."

More than two-thirds casualties were suffered by Company B in a ten-month period, of which only a limited number of days were spent in actual frontline combat. The casualties speak to how intense the fighting was during the last stages of the war. You can almost feel the sorrow in the words in the letter written home to his parents. Howard lost many friends and buddies mentioned by name in the diary, including his commanding officer.

—⁓—

12 Dec.–14 Dec.- Co Duties

15 Dec.- Leave B- 7 AM hike along the Rhine to Oberspay arr 6:30 P.M.

—⁓—

After the armistice was declared, Howard probably did not think the war was over, considering the amount of marching he did. The company was on the move east to become one of the units that was part of the American occupying force in Germany.

—⟋ⱦ⟍—

16 Dec.- Leave O- 6:30 A.M. hike through Coblens across the Maselle [Moselle] to Ochtendung arr. 4 P.M.

—⟋ⱦ⟍—

The Sixth Engineer history provides more details of how grueling the marching was before they reached Ochtendung:

> The long march had been a trying experience. Hiking day after day a distance of from fifteen to twenty-five miles, with seventy-five pounds of equipment weighing one down, over a road that climbs over endless hills and winds through forest after forest of dripping leafless trees, in rain and cold, with barely enough food to keep on going, and a bed on a hard floor at night when shoulders ached so from the pack straps that sleep was often impossible for hours, and when swollen feet had to be forced into soggy shoes upon arising, was not the enlisted man's idea of a triumphal entry into a conquered country.[47]

—⟋ⱦ⟍—

17 Dec.- Billetts for men + horses

24 Dec.- Capt. Gladding releaved [sic]. Capt. Love takes Co.

[This is the last entry Howard entered in his diary until May 20, 1919. The reason for the large gap unfortunately cannot be explained.]

—⁓—

The letters sent home after the armistice all contain the names of towns and places in Germany. The company was virtually on the march from November 14 until December 17 when they arrived in Ochtendung: "Ochtendung is a town of about two thousand inhabitants, situated in a rich farming region about halfway between Coblenz and Mayen. It was a very clean town, as German towns go, and contained sufficient accommodations to house the regiment comfortably."[48]

A letter home dated January 28, 1919, has some interesting comments as to what the American army of occupation did while in Germany waiting to return to the United States: "We have to stick around and start the crops for these people in the spring then we may stay and harvest them in the fall."

FRONT OF A POSTCARD SENT HOME TO HOWARD'S MOTHER, MRS. W. S. CLAYPOOLE, POSTMARKED FEBRUARY 15, 8 P.M., 1919.

BACK OF POSTCARD SENT HOME TO MRS. W. S.
CLAYPOOLE, DATED FEBRUARY 5, 1919.

From some of his letters, I am positive that the army of occupation did not have trouble with supplies. He also mentions regimental competition in boxing and wrestling, inter-regimental basketball, and that B Company put on a minstrel show. The troops had all kinds of activities to keep them busy and their minds off home.

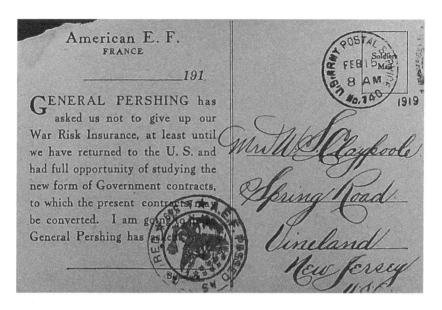

FRONT OF POSTCARD SENT HOME TO MRS. W. S. CLAYPOOLE. THE
POSTMARKED DATE APPEARS TO BE FEBRUARY 15, 1919.

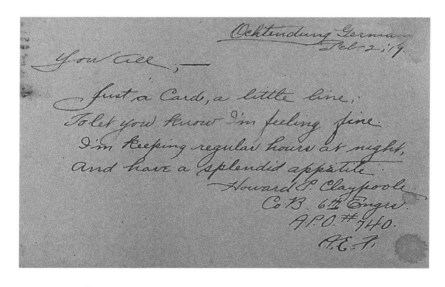

BACK OF SAME POSTCARD, WHICH APPEARS TO HAVE
BEEN WRITTEN ON FEBRUARY 2, 1919.

In a letter dated February 23, 1919, Howard mentions some of the scarce items after the war: "They have no coffee, they burn wheat like popcorn and make coffee from that, it is hard to get leather or some Of those things, soap + etc. there is no rubber at all the autos have steel tires."

The blockade was still on at this time, and the Germans were obviously feeling the pinch. Surprisingly, Howard says that souvenirs were expensive. This is amazing because of the inflation of the German currency after the war and the stability of the American dollar.

In April, Howard got leave and went to Lyon, Marseille, Nice, Monte Carlo (Monaco), and Menton near the Italian border. This was his chance to tour France and see the sights, and from his letter dated April 2, 1919, he spent sixty dollars on his travels. The travel and hotels were free for Howard.

THIS IS THE HELMET AND RIFLE SLING THAT I USED TO SEE EVERY TIME I WENT UP IN MY GRANDMOTHER'S ATTIC. UNFORTUNATELY, THERE IS NO ENTRY IN HIS DIARY EXPLAINING HOW HE OBTAINED THE UNIT CRESTS THAT WERE ATTACHED TO THE RIFLE SLING. THIS COULD HAVE BEEN HIS RIFLE SLING, AND HE TRADED FOR CRESTS THROUGHOUT HIS TIME IN FRANCE AND GERMANY. UNFORTUNATELY, WE WILL NEVER KNOW THE STORY BEHIND THE SLING.

—◊◊◊—

March 17- Division Reviewed by Gen. Pershing at Andernach. Engr work in Div area 29 men D.S. at schools.

[Here there is a large gap in the diaries. There are no entries between March 18 and May 19, 1919. Unfortunately this gap cannot be explained through letters home or other documents found in my grandmother's possession.]

20 May- Move Co. to Kripp to 4th Div area

24 May- Co. returns to Och'dung

In June, Howard was given a 3rd Division military history certificate signed by his company commander (see Appendix 9). This document is detailed with the dates he joined the regiment (October 16, 1917) and the date he landed in Europe (December 20, 1917).

The military history goes on to list his service in Europe:

- The training period in France (December 24, 1917–February 10, 1918)

- Champagne-Marne Defensive (July 15–18, 1918)

- Aisne-Marne Offensive (July 18–27, 1918)

- Training Period Gondrecourt Area (August 16–September 4, 1918)

- Saint-Mihiel Offensive (September 12–14, 1918)

- Meuse-Argonne Offensive (September 30–October 27, 1918)

- Somme Defensive (March 21–April 6, 1918)

- Army of occupation (December 16, 1918–June 10, 1919)

His military history also includes other facts:

- Citations Recommended for the *Croix de Guerre*

- Wounds: March 29, 1918, Hamel, Fr. Shell fire

- Hospital: Gen. Hosp. #18, BEF- R.C.#2. Paris-B.H. 34. Nantes

- Grades held: private, private first class, corporal

THIS WORLD WAR I VICTORY RIBBON WITH THE SIX CAMPAIGN CLASPS
WAS SENT TO ME ALONG WITH THE PURPLE HEART (FRONT AND BACK).

GEN. HOWZE PRESENTS CUP TO RIFLE TEAM
GEN. HOWZE DECORATED COLORS OF 6TH WITH BATTLE STREAMERS,
OCHTENDUNG, GERMANY
MEMORIAL DAY, 1919, OCHTENDUNG, GERMANY

—◊—

June July target range

—◊—

19 June- Leave O- 2 P.M. move to Wirnitz arr 4 P.M. standing to.

26 June- hike back to O- leave 6:30 AM arr 9:30 AM

THIS PHOTOGRAPH WAS TAKEN ON JULY 17 1919. THE PHOTO IS CAPTIONED :"6TH REGT U. S. ENGINEERS 3RD DIVISION—OCHTENDUNG GERMANY JULY -17-1919." THERE IS ALSO A NOTE THAT IS NOT QUITE CLEAR THAT SAYS: PHOTO BY BOBINGCHARK(?) AND KING MILLERSBURG, OHIO. PHOTO COURTESY OF KATHLEEN CLAYPOOLE.

3 Aug.- turn in transportation

4 Aug.- Co on D.S. at Mayen fixing box cars for Division moving

—⚬ᴍᴍ⚬—

August 5, 1919, is the last letter that Howard wrote home from Europe: "We leave here next Sunday homeward bound hope to see you soon, Howard."

—⚬ᴍᴍ⚬—

8 Aug.- Co Returns

10 Aug.- Leave O- 2 P.M. hike to Plaidt arr 5 P.M. entrain leave 7:00 P.M.

13 Aug.- Arr Brest 1 P.M. hike 3 mi to Bks [Barracks].

—⚬ᴍᴍ⚬—

The Sixth Engineer history is able to provide some detail to the two days before they boarded ship: "Here for two days [the Regiment] was subjected to physical inspections and baths and was given new clothing."[49]

—⚬ᴍᴍ⚬—

15 Aug.- Leave Bks 2:00 PM hike to fort arr about 5 P.M. load on transport Manchuria leave for U.S. 6:30 P.M.

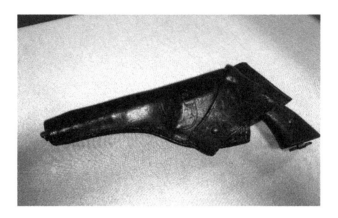

Howard brought this officer service revolver home from France. It is a Model 1917 Smith and Wesson[19] that chambered a .45 caliber round. This is in the possession of Travis Johnston, son of Kenneth Johnston, Howard's oldest grandchild (photo courtesy of Travis Johnston).

The journey home was unlike the rough seas and bad weather they experienced on the journey to France: "The voyage across the ocean consumed

19 From 1917 to 1919, Colt and Smith & Wesson produced 151,700 and 153,300 M1917s in total (respectively) under contract with the War Department for use by the American Expeditionary Force. The revolver saw prolific use by the "Doughboys" during World War I, with nearly two-thirds as many M1917s being issued and produced during the war as M1911s were. (Bruce Canfield, "America's Military Revolvers," *American Rifleman*, May 1997, https://www.americanrifleman.org/content/america-s-military-revolvers/, accessed June 3, 2020)

ten pleasurably spent days, as the ocean was very calm, the weather serene, the chow good, and entertainment every evening."[50]

"The Statue of Liberty was sighted at five o'clock in the afternoon of the 26th, and by eight that evening the regiment had arrived at Camp Merritt, where it was at once unceremoniously demobilized."[51]

—⚬—

25 Aug.- Arr at Hoboken about 6 P.M. go to Camp Merritt

28 Aug.- Leave Merritt for Dix arr about noon

29 Aug.- Get the glad papers and start home a free man!!

—⚬—

Howard also had $103.55 in his pocket when he left for home. His discharge papers indicate that his final payment included a $50.00 bonus. On the papers there is a section that says "PAYMENT OF BONUS," and stamped just below that is the word "RECOMMENDED."

From Fort Dix to his home in Vineland was approximately fifty-one miles. Anyone traveling home from a deployment knows that this trip probably seemed like an eternity to Howard as he returned home. I am sure his mother and father were happy to see their son, who had been gone for almost two years, who they knew had been wounded, and who was very fortunate to be one of the lucky ones who returned *home*.

PICTURE OF HOWARD CLAYPOOLE AND EUGENE BOSTWICK
CIRCA 1939 AT BOSTWICK'S HOME IN NEW JERSEY. BOSTWICK IS
MENTIONED SEVERAL TIMES IN HOWARD'S DIARY (PHOTO COURTESY
OF JEFFREY CLAYPOOLE, GRANDSON OF HOWARD CLAYPOOLE).

EPILOGUE

After the war, Howard ended up moving into his uncle William and aunt Kate Dawson's house and was the head shipping clerk at the Claremont Paper Company in Claremont, New Hampshire. Majel Evans went to work as a secretary at the paper company in February 1923. She met Howard through office contact. Family history and folklore says that Majel approached Howard and asked him out on a date.

They were married on May 8, 1926, at 2:00 p.m. at Majel's parents' house (David H. Evans and Sarah Alice Barrell Evans), the Reverend Gill presiding. My grandmother notes that they had wedding cake and ice cream. Majel was twenty-five, and Howard was thirty-three years old.

They took over the Evans & Evans family store in Hartland, Vermont. They ran the store together as a family business for the next thirteen years. Howard and Majel welcomed their first child, David Winfield Claypoole, on July 15, 1927, in Windsor, Vermont. A daughter, Alice Jane Claypoole, was born on October 17, 1928. Their third child, Patricia Louise Claypoole, was born on November 21, 1939.

PHOTOGRAPH OF B COMPANY ENGINEERS 1939 3RD DIVISION REUNION.
LEFT TO RIGHT: HOWARD CLAYPOOLE, EUGENE BOSTWICK, JOE HAYNES,
AND GEORGE CROWLEY (PHOTOGRAPH COURTESY OF JEFFREY CLAYPOOLE).

6TH ENGINEERS AT THE 3RD DIVISION CONVENTION HELD AT THE
SAINT GEORGE HOTEL IN BROOKLYN, NEW YORK. THIS WAS THE LAST
REUNION HOWARD WOULD ATTEND. HIS WIFE, MAJEL, WENT TO THIS
REUNION WITH HIM. HOWARD IS LOCATED IN THE SECOND ROW, SECOND
IN FROM THE RIGHT (PHOTO COURTESY OF JEFFREY CLAYPOOLE).

In an application for federal employment (standard form no. 57),
Majel notes she was in "charge of major portion of buying merchandise,
handled all bookkeeping accounts, made out statements, payroll, kept
social security, and income tax records."

There are family stories that Howard had issues with his wounds
even after the war. In a letter my grandmother wrote in February 1939,
she stated: "The groceries are in so I feel I must stop and help Howard.
This shoveling [of snow] is hard on him, and his tummy—he is ready
for bed right now."

Howard Claypoole went into the hospital for appendicitis in January 1940. He never left the hospital and died on January 17, 1940. He was forty-six years old.

This is his obituary:

HARTLAND
Death of Howard P. Claypoole

Hartland has lost one of its most beloved citizens in the death of Howard P. Claypoole, which occurred at the Windsor Hospital at 8 o'clock Wednesday evening, January 17, after a week's illness following an emergency appendectomy.

Howard was born in Bridgeton, NJ, Jan 30, 1893, and spent his boyhood in Vineland, NJ. He enlisted in the army, Oct 9, 1917, and served overseas with the 3rd Division, 6th Engineers until he returned to Vineland, Aug 29th, 1919. After that he was employed in Claremont, NH, until May 1926 when he came to Hartland, following his marriage May 8, 1926, and entered the store of Evans & Evans of which he was manager.

He was a member of the Masonic Lodge in Windsor, and of the American Legion, Post No. 48 of Hartland.

He is survived by his widow Majel (Evans) Claypoole, and three children, David, Alice Jean, and Patricia Louise, the youngest only 8 weeks old; also by his mother Mrs. Jane Claypoole, and brother Clarence Claypoole, both of Vineland; and by an uncle W. M. Dawson of Claremont.

Funeral services for Mr. Claypoole were held Sunday afternoon at the brick church. The house was filled to overflowing and the balcony, extra chairs and standing room were all taken. The flag-draped casket was banked with flowers, and the flags of the United States and of the American Legion stood at the ends of the platform each one softly glowing from the rays of a beautiful lamp placed near it. The speaker was Rev. Dr. William Forkell who offered a prayer and several poems. The organist was Robert H. Blondin of Windsor, who played a number of hymns and also "O' Sweet Mystery of Love," Howard's favorite selection. The bearers were Walter F. Hatch, Webb T. Hatch, Frank Bement, Roger W. Flanagan, Alonzo A. Martin, all of Hartland, and George Finefska of Claremont, NH.

The Hartland Post No. 48, American Legion, and Auxiliary Unit, attended in a body, and at the grave a salute was given by the firing squad. It was planned for "Taps" to be played, Russell Bement, son of past Commander Frank Bement, found his trumpet frozen.

David Claypoole, Howard's son was ill in bed suffering from rheumatic fever, and unable to attend.

Relatives and friends from out of town were as follows: Mrs. Jane M. Claypoole, Clarence Claypoole, of Vineland, NJ; Mr. and Mrs. W. C. Dawson, Richard Dawson, Claremont, NH; Edgar Barrell, Mrs. Sumner Smith, Phillip Smith, Charles Clark, Milford, Conn; Miss Lemoyne Evans, Utica, NY; Mr. and Mrs. Afton Howlett, Warner, NH; Mr. and Mrs. Earl Davis, Floyd Davis, Mr. and Mrs. Alfred Sherwin, Windsor, Vt.; Mr. and Mrs. Gordon Noyes, Bellows Falls; George Finefska, Miss Sarah Edith Bryant, Miss Alice Clearly, Miss Edith Bryant, Mr. and Mrs. Howard Pierce, Claremont, NH.

Mr. and Mrs. D. H. Evans were called home from Florida where they had gone to spend the winter.

—∿—

After Howard's death on January 17, Majel was unable to run the store with three small children. On top of that, her son was suffering from rheumatic fever, and the store shut its doors permanently in April 1940.

My grandmother told me after Howard died, she burned all of his uniforms.

Majel Claypoole first worked for the War Department in Rutland. A War Department personnel memo notes that, effective March 16, 1942, her probationary employment was over and she was classified as a "Junior Clerk-Stenographer CAF-2 at $1440 per annum, Quartermaster Corps of the Army QM, Rutland, Vermont." She worked for various government agencies until she retired from government service after working twenty-nine years for the US Forest Service. She died in 1991.

David Claypoole served in the army at the end of World War II and used the GI Bill to obtain an civil engineering degree from the University of Vermont, where he met his future wife, Hester Brown. They were married in 1953. They had four children: Kathleen Joan, Jeffrey David, Janet Eileen, and Steven David. David W. Claypoole passed away in 2006.

Alice Jane Claypoole (known as Jane) married a World War II veteran, Ulric Johnston, in 1946. They had four children: Kenneth Howard (deceased in 2019), Elric (Ricky) Scott, Barbara Jane, and Karen Joan. Jane Johnston passed away in 2021.

Patricia Claypoole married Paul E. Hill in 1958 and had three children: Kimberly Jean, Gregory Scott, and Howard Paul (who died shortly after his birth). Kim and Greg were adopted by Patricia's second husband, John E. Valloch. Patricia passed away on May 10, 2013, six days after attending her son's retirement ceremony from the United States Army Reserve after thirty years of service.

There are many unanswered questions from reading the diary and reviewing all the items Howard came home with from his time in the army and his service in France. How did he get the rifle sling with the unit crests? How did he get the service revolver that was only issued to officers? Where did he get the two French bayonets? Where did he get the engraved shell that he brought home from France? Why was there a large gap in the diary and diary entries? I will never know the answers to these questions, but I am glad that he kept a diary to share with his family and that my grandmother did not throw out all of these items that are on display in this book.

So this brings to an end the story of Howard Claypoole. He served gallantly in the army and survived being wounded and being operated on twice in primitive hospital conditions. He rejoined his unit and served in five more major engagements. He was fortunate to survive the war when so many in his unit did not return home.

He was able to marry and raise a family for thirteen-plus years while running a general store in Hartland, Vermont. His untimely death left his wife in a difficult position that she also was able to endure to raise three children. Family lore says that my mother, Patricia Mitiguy, was a gift from God to keep her busy instead of grieving over the early death of her husband.

HOWARD CLAYPOOLE, CIRCA 1939. THIS PHOTOGRAPH WAS
BESIDE MY GRANDMOTHER'S BED FOR ALL MY YEARS GROWING
UP. I WAS GIVEN THE PHOTOGRAPH AFTER MY GRANDMOTHER
PASSED AWAY. IT SITS ON AN END TABLE BESIDE MY BED.

I believe if my grandfather could tell us what he thought of his legacy as a father and a husband, it would be that he was very proud of his wife for the way she raised their three children after his death. I am sure he would have loved all his grandchildren and been a great grandfather to all of us. All of the grandchildren are proud that their grandfather served in the Great War, returned, and was a respected member of the community where he lived. He is an inspiration to all of us for the way he lived his life without bringing the war home with him. We all wish we knew him, but we carry around a part of him with us every day.

EVANS & EVANS FAMILY STORE WITH MAJEL'S PARENTS IN FRONT OF THE STORE,
DAVID EVANS AND HIS WIFE, SARAH ALICE (BARRELL) EVANS, CIRCA 1920.

PHOTOGRAPH OF THE FRONT OF THE EVANS & EVANS STORE LOCATED
IN HARTLAND, VERMONT (PHOTO COURTESY OF RICK JOHNSTON

ONE OF THE LAST KNOWN PHOTOS OF MY GRANDFATHER
HOWARD CLAYPOOLE BEFORE HE DIED, CIRCA 1939.

MAJEL CLAYPOOLE WITH HER SON DAVID, DAUGHTER ALICE
JANE, AND MY MOTHER, PATRICIA, CIRCA 1944.

GOLD COIN HOWARD BROUGHT HOME FROM GERMANY. THIS COIN WAS GIVEN TO MY MOTHER, PATRICIA MITIGUY, WHO HAD IT CLAD AND MADE INTO A NECKLACE.

THE FRONT OF THE COIN IS THE GERMAN KING AND SAYS
WILHELM DEUTSCHER KAISER KONIG V. PRUESSEN,
AND THE OBVERSE SAYS DEUTSCHES REICH 1875 10 MARK.

WHAT IS THE INDEPENDENT ORDER OF ODD FELLOWS?

This organization is mentioned in Howard's diary entries of October 25 and 26, 1917. When I first transcribed the diaries back in 1983, I did not investigate what IOOF stood for or what it meant, but after doing subsequent research and finding the charm in his old coin purse, my curiosity was aroused. What is the IOOF? The charm he had engraved with his name says: "Grand Lodge Independent Order Of Odd Fellows New Jersey." The coin has the number 299, and in the middle it is engraved with "H. P. Claypoole."

The IOOF still exists today. They have a website, and under their mission states:

> As an organization, the Independent Order of Odd Fellows aims to provide a framework that promotes personal and social development. Lodge degrees and activities aim to improve and elevate every person to a higher, nobler plane; to extend sympathy and aid to those in need, making their burdens lighter, relieving the darkness of despair; to war against vice in every form, and to be a great moral power and influence for the good of humanity.

For members, the degrees in Odd Fellowship emphasizes a leaving of the old life and the start of a better one, of welcoming travelers, and of helping those in need.

The command of the IOOF is to "visit the sick, relieve the distressed, bury the dead and educate the orphan." Specifically, IOOF today are dedicated to the following purposes:

- To improve and elevate the character of mankind by promoting the principles of friendship, love, truth, faith, hope, charity and universal justice.

- To help make the world a better place to live by aiding each other, the community, the less fortunate, the youth, the elderly, the environment and the community in every way possible.

- To promote good will and harmony amongst peoples and nations through the principle of universal fraternity, holding the belief that all men and women regardless of race, nationality, religion, social status, gender, rank and station are brothers and sisters.[52]

HOWARD CLAYPOOLE'S PURPLE HEART

During World War I, there was not an official Purple Heart as we know it today. Soldiers who were wounded in combat were awarded a wound chevron to their uniform. That was the only way a soldier could show that he had been wounded.

> What most soldiers, and most Americans, do not realize, however, is that the Purple Heart is a unique military award. First, it is the oldest U.S. military decoration; General George Washington awarded the first purple-colored heart-shaped badges to soldiers who fought in the Continental Army during the American Revolution. Second, until World War II, the Purple Heart was exclusively an Army decoration and, with rare exceptions, only soldiers received it; the Navy and Marine Corps lacked the authority to award it to sea service personnel. Finally, the Purple Heart is the only decoration awarded without regard to any person's favor or approval; any soldier, sailor, airman or marine who sheds blood in defense of the nation is automatically awarded the Purple Heart. What follows is a history of this unique decoration and some of its soldier recipients.

On February 22, 1932, the Army announced in General Orders No. 3 that "the Purple Heart, established by General George Washington in 1782" would be "awarded to persons who, while serving in the Army of the United States, perform any singularly meritorious act of extraordinary fidelity or essential service." Then, in a parenthetical in this announcement, the Army published the following sentence: "A wound, which necessitates treatment by a medical officer, and which is received in action with an enemy of the United States, or as a result of an act of such enemy, may...be construed as resulting from a singularly meritorious act of essential service." This meant that the Purple Heart was an award for high-level service, but it also meant that an individual serving "in the Army" who was wounded in action, could also be awarded the Purple Heart. Not all wounds, however, qualified for the new decoration; the wound had to be serious enough that it "necessitated" medical treatment.

From 1932 until the outbreak of World War II, the Army awarded some 78,000 Purple Hearts to living veterans and active duty soldiers who had either been wounded in action or had been awarded General Pershing's certificate for meritorious service during World War I. The latter was a printed certificate signed by Pershing that read "for exceptionally meritorious and conspicuous services." While the vast majority of Purple Hearts were issued to men who had fought in Europe in 1917 and 1918, a small number of soldiers who had been wounded in earlier conflicts, including the Civil War, Indian Wars, and Spanish-American War, applied for and were awarded the Purple Heart.[53]

My grandfather never submitted for a Purple Heart after it became an award for wounds suffered during World War I. In the summer of 2015, I decided that I would submit paperwork documenting that Howard Claypoole earned a Purple Heart during his service in France.

I submitted:

- the order stating he was allowed to wear the wound chevron

- the 3rd Division service document signed by a commissioned officer stating where he was wounded

- discharge paperwork including "wounds received—Somme Defensive March, 1918"

- newspaper clippings stating "local boy wounded in action"

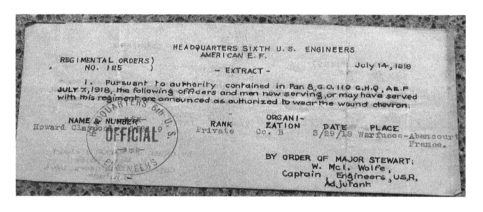

WOUND CHEVRON ORDER DATED JULY 14, 1918.

In mid-July 2015, I received his orders, a Purple Heart certificate, a Purple Heart, his World War I victory medal with campaign clasps, and a lapel pin. I contacted the human resources decoration department by telephone and asked if there was any way that I could get two more certificates, so each of Howard's children would have a certificate. The person I spoke with told me, "Unfortunately, we can only give out one certificate. You can, however, make high-quality copies of the certificate you do have." I was disappointed but understood the rationale behind that decision. One week later, I received two more original certificates in the mail. I kept one, gave one to the oldest surviving child of David Claypoole, and one to Aunt Jane, the only surviving child of Howard Claypoole.

LINEAGE AND HONORS INFORMATION AS OF APRIL 25, 2015

6TH ENGINEER BATTALION
(OAK)

- Organized 31 December 1861 in the Regular Army at Washington, DC, from new and existing companies of engineers as a provisional engineer battalion (constituted 28 July 1866 as the Battalion of Engineers)

- Expanded 14 March – 7 June 1901 to form the 1st and 2nd Battalions of Engineers (2nd Battalion of Engineers—hereafter separate lineage)

- 1st Battalion of Engineers expanded, reorganized, and redesignated 1 July 1916 as the 1st Engineer Regiment

- 1st Regiment of Engineers expanded 15 May 1917 to form the 1st, 6th, and 7th Regiments of Engineers (1st and 7th Regiments of Engineers—hereafter separate lineages)

- 6th Regiment of Engineers redesignated 29 August 1917 as the 6th Engineers

- Assigned 1 October 1917 to the 3rd Division

- Regiment broken up 12 October 1939 and its elements reorganized and redesignated as follows:

    - 1st Battalion as the 6th Engineer Battalion, an element of the 6th Division (later redesignated as the 6th Infantry Division)

    - (Headquarters and Headquarters and Service Company disbanded; 2nd Battalion as the 10th Engineer Battalion—hereafter separate lineage)

- 6th Engineer Battalion reorganized and redesignated 9 April 1942 as the 6th Engineer Motorized Battalion

- Reorganized and redesignated 1 May 1943 as the 6th Engineer Combat Battalion

- Inactivated 10 January 1949 in Korea

- Activated 4 October 1950 at Fort Ord, California

- Inactivated 3 April 1956 at Fort Ord, California

- Redesignated 15 May 1958 as the 6th Engineer Battalion and relieved from assignment to the 6th Infantry Division; concurrently activated at West Point, New York

- Inactivated 1 May 1966 at West Point, New York

- Headquarters and Headquarters Company, 6th Engineer Battalion, redesignated 15 June 1967 as the 6th Engineer Company, assigned to the 11th Infantry Brigade, and activated at Schofield Barracks, Hawaii

- Inactivated 15 January 1968 in Vietnam, and relieved from assignment to the 11th Infantry Brigade

- Redesignated 17 August 1988 as Headquarters and Headquarters Company, 6th Engineer Battalion, assigned to the 6th Infantry Division, and activated at Fort Wainwright, Alaska (organic elements concurrently activated)

- Inactivated 15 June 1994 at Fort Wainwright, Alaska, and relieved from assignment to the 6th Infantry Division

- Headquarters and Headquarters Company activated 16 October 2008 at Fort Richardson, Alaska (Support Company concurrently constituted and activated)

- Assigned 16 October 2014 to the 4th Brigade Combat Team, 25th Infantry Division (Support Company concurrently inactivated and lettered companies activated)

CAMPAIGN PARTICIPATION CREDIT

- Civil War

  - Peninsula

  - Antietam

  - Fredericksburg

  - Chancellorsville

  - Wilderness

  - Spotsylvania

- Cold Harbor

- Petersburg

- Appomattox

- Virginia 1863

- Philippine Insurrection

  - Streamer without inscription

- World War I

  - Somme Defensive

  - Champagne-Marne

  - Aisne-Marne

  - St. Mihiel

  - Meuse-Argonne

  - Champagne 1918

- World War II

  - New Guinea (with arrowhead)

  - Luzon (with arrowhead)

  - Vietnam

- Counteroffensive, Phase III

DECORATIONS

- French *Croix de Guerre* with Palm, World War I, streamer embroidered CHAMPAGNE-MARNE AISNE-MARNE

- Philippine Presidential Unit Citation, streamer embroidered 17 OCTOBER 1944 TO 4 JULY 1945

BY ORDER OF THE SECRETARY OF THE ARMY: RICHARD W. STEWART, PhD Chief of Military History

https://history.army.mil/html/forcestruc/lineages/branches/eng/0006enbn.htm

APPENDIX 6

6TH ENGINEER
COMMENDATIONS

HEADQUARTERS THIRD DIVISION
AMERICAN EXPEDITIONARY FORCES,
USAPO 740 — 3 JANUARY 1919.

GENERAL ORDERS,)

NO. 67　　)

　　　The following is published as a matter of record, being letters of commendations received by the 6th U.S. Engineers, while that regiment was on duty with the 4th and 5th British Armies:

Colonel Hodges　　　　　　　　　　　Fifth Army
Commanding 6th Regiment　　　　　　S.G. 72
United States Engineers.　　　　　　1st April, 1918.

　　　The Army Commander wishes to record officially his appreciation of the excellent work your regiment has done in assisting the British Army to resist the enemy's powerful offensive during the last ten days.

　　　I fully realise that it has been largely due to your assistance that the enemy is checked, and I rely on you to assist us still further during the few days which arestill to come before I shall be able to relaieve you in the line.

　　　I consider your work in the line to be greatly enhanced by the fact that for six weeks previous to taking your place in the front line your men had been working at such high pressure erecting heavy bridges over the Somme.

　　　My best congratulations and warm thanks to you all.

　　　　　　　　(Signed) Rawlinson,
　　　　　　　　　　General, Commanding V Army.

G.A. 126. 31/3

　　　1.　The following message has been received from the Army Commander: "Please convey my warmest thanks to 1st Cavalry Division and General's two Brigades of 2nd Cavalry Division for their successes of yesterday. They have rendered valuable services and I am deeply grateful to them, I trust their losses have not been very severe."

　　　2.　The Division Commander wishes to add his heartiest congratulations and thanks to all ranks for the magnificient manner in which they beat off all attacks on the 30 th March.

　　　　　　(Signed)　　S.F. Muspratt. Lt. Col. G.S.
　　　　　　　　　　　　1st Cavalry Division.

O.C. U.S. Engineer Battalion.
G.A. 126/1, 1/4

As the U.S. Engineer Battalion was fighting with the 1st Cavalry Division in the line on the 30th March, the Army Commander's congratulatory message applies to them equally with units of the 1st Cavalry Division.

It has been brought to my notice that the men under command fought most gallantly alongside the British Cavalry.

I am most grateful to you and the unit under your command for the invaluable assistance you gave us on the 30th March 1918.

Please convey my thanks and congratulations to all ranks.

(Signed)   R. L. MULLENS, Major General,
            Commanding 1st Cavalry Division.

To Lieutenant Colonel HODGES,
O.C. 6th Regiment,
U.S. Engineers.

C.R.E.
Corps Troops
AUSTRALIAN CORPS.

I should be glad if you would convey to Major LARKIN and the officers and men of A and C Companies of your Regiment my appreciation of the work they have carried out in this area under my direction.

The behavior of the men while on night work, and on more than one occasion under what can called fairly heavy firing, was excellent.

The keenness of the officers to carry out the work in a thoroughly efficient manner gave me the greatest pleasure and I consider the result of their efforts was entirely satisfactory.

The night work done by them in the BUIRRE District and the last portion of entrenching at DOURS was og high standard. The wiring developed a rapidity comparable with some of the best units I have in this area, and intelligence shown in laying out an entirely new class of wiring beyond DOURS and LA NEUVILLE was most gratifying.

I especially mention to you Captain HEAVEY, Lieut. HANLOW and Lieut. CRANE, and I am sure Major LARKIN has been satisfied with the progress generally shown. He was indefatigable in assisting the work and my special thanks are due to him for his efforts.

(Signed)   J.H.NICHOLSON.
           Lieut. Col. A. E.
           C. R.C.
           AUSTRALIAN CORPS TROOPS.

APPENDIX 7

Official promotion order dated July 18 (promotion
effective November 10, 1918).

APPENDIX 8

THIS IS THE CASE THAT WAS GIVEN TO CPL. HOWARD CLAYPOOLE WHEN
HE WAS DISCHARGED. HIS DISCHARGE DOCUMENT WAS INSIDE THIS
BLACK FOLDER WHEN I WAS GIVEN MY GRANDFATHER'S BELONGINGS.

Honorable Discharge from The United States Army

TO ALL WHOM IT MAY CONCERN:

This is to Certify, That Howard P Claypoole
†158119 Corporal C B 6th Engineers
THE UNITED STATES ARMY, *as a* TESTIMONIAL OF HONEST AND FAITHFUL SERVICE, *is hereby* HONORABLY DISCHARGED *from the military service of the* UNITED STATES *by reason of* ‡ Circular 106 W D 1918
Said Howard P Claypoole *was born in* Bridgeton*, in the State of* New Jersey
When enlisted he was 24 *years of age and by occupation a* agent
He had blue *eyes,* brown *hair,* ruddy *complexion, and was* 5 *feet* 4½ *inches in height.*
Given under my hand at Camp Dix N J *this* 29 *day of* Aug*, one thousand nine hundred and* nineteen

John N Foos
Major U.S.A.
Commanding.

Form No. 525, A. G. O.
Oct. 9-18.

2—8184

* Insert name, Christian name first; e. g., "John Doe."
† Insert Army serial number, grade, company and regiment or arm or corps or department; a. g., "1,520,309"; "Corporal, Company A, 1st Infantry"; "Sergeant, Quartermaster Corps"; "Sergeant, First Class, Medical Department."
‡ If discharged prior to expiration of service, give number, date, and source of order or full description of authority therefor.

HONORABLE DISCHARGE FROM THE UNITED STATES
ARMY AND ENLISTMENT RECORD (FRONT)

ENLISTMENT RECORD.

Name: *Howard P. Claypoole* Grade: *Cpl*

Enlisted, or *Inducted,* *Oct 9* , 191*7*, at *Atlantic City N J*

Serving in *First* enlistment period at date of discharge.

Prior service: * *None*

Noncommissioned officer: *Apld Cpl 11/10/18*

Marksmanship, gunner qualification or rating: † *Marksman 7/6/9. R.O. 130.*

Horsemanship: *Not mounted*

Battles, engagements, skirmishes, expeditions *Somme Def 3/21/20 Champagne Marne Def 7/15/18 - Aisne Marne Off 7/18/27 St Mihiel Off (Corp troop) 9/12/9/14 - Meuse Argonne Off 9/30/ 11 7/1918*

Knowledge of any vocation: *R R Agent*

Wounds received in service: *Mar 28/18 - Somme Def - Shrapnel*

Physical condition when discharged: *Good*

Typhoid prophylaxis completed *7/26/9*

Paratyphoid prophylaxis completed *5/26/19.*

Married or single: *Single*

Character: *Excellent*

Remarks: *Served in France Germany left US 1st England in US 7/26/9 Army of Occ 9/16 to 9/19*

Signature of soldier: *Howard P. Claypoole*

Howard Clark Jr

Captain USA

Commanding *Dis Unit #4*

† Give company and regiment or corps or department, with positive dates of serving each enlistment.
† Give date of qualification or rating and number, date, and source of order announcing same.

STATE OF NEW JERSEY
FIELD AGENT
JUL 26 1921
PAYMENT OF BONUS

HONORABLE DISCHARGE FROM THE UNITED STATES
ARMY AND ENLISTMENT RECORD (BACK)

APPENDIX 9

ITEMS GIVEN TO ME BY MY GRANDMOTHER MRS. HOWARD P. CLAYPOOLE:
3RD DIVISION PATCH, PRIVATE AND CORPORAL DOG TAG (BOTH OF WHICH
INCLUDE HIS SERVICE NUMBER, 158119), EUROPEAN CAMPAIGN RIBBON,
FRENCH FIVE-FRANC COIN DATED 1876, AND HIS MARKSMANSHIP BADGE.

APPENDIX 10

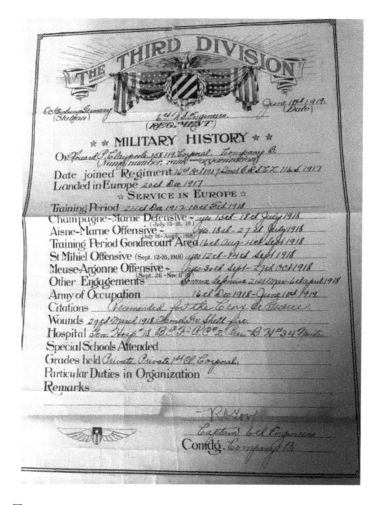

THE ABOVE DOCUMENT WAS ONE OF THE DOCUMENTS I SUBMITTED
FOR MY GRANDFATHER'S PURPLE HEART. AS AN ORIGINAL SOURCE
DOCUMENT, SIGNED BY A COMMISSIONED OFFICER, IT WAS KEY TO
SUBSTANTIATE THAT MY GRANDFATHER WAS WOUNDED.

APPENDIX 11

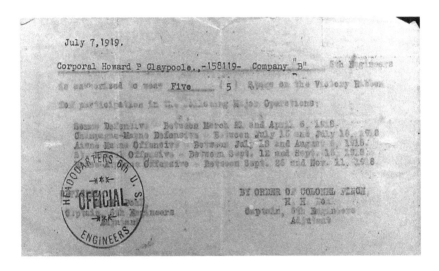

THIS ORDER AUTHORIZES HOWARD CLAYPOOLE TO
WEAR FIVE STARS ON HIS VICTORY RIBBON.

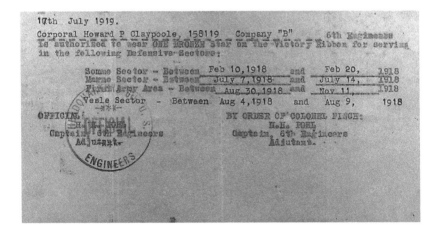

THIS ORDER ALLOWS HOWARD TO WEAR A SIXTH STAR ON HIS VICTORY RIBBON.

APPENDIX 12

THIS WAS THE HELMET THAT I USED TO SEE IN MY GRANDMOTHER'S ATTIC. NOTE PAINTED 3RD DIVISION PATCH ON THE HELMET.

APPENDIX 13

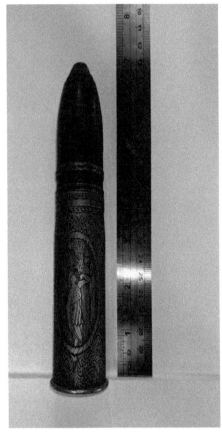

THIS IS TRENCH ART INSCRIBED ON A BRASS GERMAN SHELL CASING THAT
HOWARD CLAYPOOLE BROUGHT HOME FROM FRANCE. THE SHELL IS ENGRAVED
ON THE FRONT WITH "H. P. CLAYPOOLE," THE DATE HE ARRIVED IN FRANCE,
THE BATTLES HE PARTICIPATED IN, AND THE DATE HE RETURNED HOME
FROM FRANCE. THE BACK SIDE SHOWS LADY LIBERTY WITH AN EAGLE
PERCHED ON HER LEFT ARM AND A SWORD IN HER RIGHT HAND (PHOTOGRAPH
COURTESY OF STEVEN CLAYPOOLE, GRANDSON OF HOWARD CLAYPOOLE).

APPENDIX 14
BAYONET PICTURES

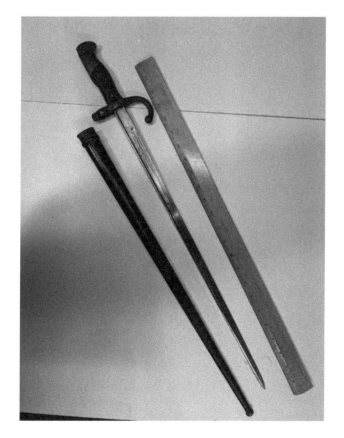

ONE OF THE BAYONETS HOWARD CLAYPOOLE BROUGHT HOME
FROM FRANCE. THE BLADE IS INSCRIBED "L. DERRY PARIS"
(PHOTOGRAPH COURTESY OF STEVEN CLAYPOOLE).

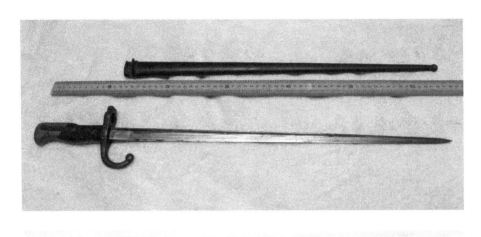

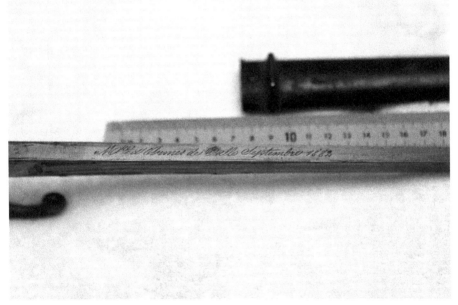

This bayonet was also brought home by Howard Claypoole and is of unknown origin, but it is engraved with "Mre d'Armes de Tulle Septembre 1882" (photo courtesy of Jeffrey Claypoole).

APPENDIX 15

WAR DEPARTMENT MEMO NOTIFYING MAJEL E. CLAYPOOLE OF HER
HIRING AS A JUNIOR CLERK-STENOGRAPHER. THIS OCCURRED ROUGHLY
14 MONTHS AFTER THE DEATH OF HOWARD CLAYPOOLE.

APPENDIX 16

THE ORIGINAL VA GRAVESTONE IS NO LONGER VISIBLE. IT WAS
REPLACED BY A LARGE FAMILY GRAVESTONE THAT NOW COVERS
THIS ORIGINAL MARKER FOR MY GRANDFATHER.

CRESTS FROM THE RIFLE SLING

The Gloucestershire Regiment Infantry

"Sixteen battalions of the regiment saw active service in France during World War I and Flanders, Italy, Gallipoli, Egypt, Mesopotamia, Persia, and Salonika, losing a total of 8,100 men and winning seventy-two different battle honors. Four awards of the Victoria Cross (VC) were made to soldiers serving with the regiment. The wartime battalions were disbanded as the war ended, and just before the Second World War, two of the territorial battalions were repurposed and ceased to have any affiliation with the regiment." ("Gloucestershire Regiment," Wikipedia, https://en.wikipedia.org/wiki/Gloucestershire_Regiment, accessed December 8, 2021)

The Royal Regiment of Artillery

[2]

The Royal Regiment of Artillery, commonly referred to as the Royal Artillery (RA) and colloquially known as "The Gunners," is the artillery arm of the British Army. The Royal Regiment of Artillery comprises thirteen Regular Army regiments, King's Troop Royal Horse Artillery, and five Army Reserve regiments." ("Royal Artillery," Wikipedia, https://en.wikipedia.org/wiki/Royal_Artillery, accessed December 8, 2021).

The Gordon Highlanders

"The Gordon Highlanders was a line infantry regiment of the British Army that existed for 113 years from 1881 until 1994, when it was amalgamated with the Queen's Own Highlanders (Seaforth and Camerons) to form the Highlanders (Seaforth, Gordons, and Camerons). Although the Gordon Highlanders had existed as the 92nd (Gordon Highlanders) Regiment of Foot since 1794, the actual Gordon Highlanders Regiment was formed in 1881 by amalgamation of the 75th (Stirlingshire) Regiment of Foot and 92nd (Gordon Highlanders) Regiment of Foot." ("Gordon Highlanders," Wikipedia, https://en.wikipedia. org/wiki/Gordon_Highlanders, accessed December 8, 2021).

The Newfoundland Regiment

"Governor Davidson strongly felt that the Newfoundland Regiment deserved special recognition for its actions during the battles of <u>Ypres</u> and <u>Cambrai</u>. His request to the British government to add the prefix Royal to the regiment's name was granted, and George V bestowed the regiment with the prefix in December 1917._This was the only time during the First World War that this honor was given and only the third time in the history of the British Army that it has been given during a time of war." ("Royal Newfoundland Regiment," Wikipedia, https:// en.wikipedia.org/wiki/Royal_Newfoundland_Regiment, accessed December 8, 2021).

The Machine Gun Corps

"The Machine Gun Corps (MGC) was a corps of the British Army, formed in October 1915 in response to the need for more effective use of machine guns on the Western Front in the First World War. The Heavy Branch of the MGC was the first to use tanks in combat and was subsequently turned into the Tank Corps, later called the Royal Tank Regiment. The MGC remained in existence after the war until it was disbanded in 1922." ("Machine

Gun Corps," Wikipedia, https://en.wikipedia.org/wiki/ Machine Gun Corps, accessed December 8, 2021).

The 43rd Battalion (Cameron Highlanders of Canada)

"The 43rd Battalion (Cameron Highlanders of Canada), CEF...was authorized on 7 November 1914 and embarked for Britain on 1 June 1915. It disembarked in France on 22 February 1916, where it fought as part of the 9th Infantry Brigade, 3rd Canadian Division in France and Flanders until the end of the war. The battalion was disbanded on 15 September 1920." ("43rd Battalion (Cameron Highlanders of Canada), CEF," Wikipedia, https://en.wikipedia. org/wiki/43rd Battalion (Cameron Highlanders of Canada), CEF, accessed December 8, 2021).

The Manchester Regiment

"The Manchester Regiment was a line infantry regiment of the British Army in existence from 1881 until 1958. The regiment was created during the 1881 Childers Reforms by the amalgamation of the 63rd (West Suffolk) Regiment of Foot and the 96th Regiment of Foot as the 1st and 2nd battalions; the 6th Royal Lancashire Militia became the 3rd (Reserve) and 4th (Extra Reserve) battalions and the Volunteer battalions became the 5th, 6th, 7th, 8th, 9th, and 10th battalions." ("Manchester Regiment," Wikipedia, https://en.wikipedia.org/wiki/Manchester_Regiment, accessed December 8, 2021).

The Green Howards (Alexandra, Princess of Wales's Own Yorkshire Regiment

"The Green Howards (Alexandra, Princess of Wales's Own Yorkshire Regiment), frequently known as the Yorkshire Regiment until the 1920s, was a line infantry regiment of the British Army, in the King's Division. Raised in 1688, it served under various titles until it was amalgamated with the Prince of Wales's Own Regiment of Yorkshire and the Duke of Wellington's Regiment (West Riding), all Yorkshire-based regiments in the King's Division, to form the Yorkshire Regiment (14th/15th, 19th and 33rd/76th Foot) on 6 June 2006." ("Green Howards," Wikipedia, https://en.wikipedia.org/wiki/Green_Howards, accessed December 8, 2021)

2nd South African Infantry Regiment

"The infantry regiments [to include the Second South African Infantry Regiment] were raised with men from the four provinces of the Union: the 2nd Regiment troops were from Natal and Orange Free State....The Regiment was deployed to France where it capture the village of Longueval and was deployed in the adjacent Delville Wood on the 15th July 1916. The regiment then served with the Brigade at Arras during April 1917 and was part of the offensive at Ypres and Passchendale in September 1917, at Marrieres Wood in March 1918, at Messines in April 1918 and finally at Le Cateau in October 1918."

("2nd South African Infantry Regiment," Military History Fandom, https://military-history.fandom.com/wiki/2nd_South_African_Infantry_Regiment, accessed December 8, 2021).

The officers and men of the [Army Service Corps] were the unsung heroes of the British Army during the Great War. Soldiers can not fight without food, equipment and ammunition. They can not move without horses or vehicles. It was the ASCs job to provide them. https://www.longlongtrail.co.uk/army/regiments-and-corps/the army service corp

ACKNOWLEDGMENTS

This book could not have been written at all if my grandmother Majel E. Claypoole had not saved Howard's diaries and all the myriad other items that he brought home from France. Without her saving these items, there would be no book to attempt to honor my grandfather. My mother was also instrumental in the writing of my college paper where I transcribed the diaries into a research paper.

I also have to thank all the people who have helped me turn the college paper into a book. Kind friends read my extremely rough draft of a book and gave me guidance and help with research. Thank you, Justin Orabona, author Michael Blackwood (also known as the CFB Wizard, or your favorite college football prognosticator), Katherine Campbell, Mark Gerges, high school classmate and author Susan Thatcher, and Michael Farmer, for your support in writing this book. I would also be remiss if I did not thank Alexandra Lapointe and the incredible editing team at Palmetto Publishing for their help in making this dream a reality.

Family is *always* important, and they have contributed much to this book with pictures, artifacts, and memories passed on through family members. A special thank you to Ricky Johnston, Travis Johnston, Kathleen Claypoole, Jeffrey Claypoole, Steven Claypoole, and Kimberly Prescott for contributing photographs of artifacts and historical documents that are in their possession.

A special thank you to Skylar Dennis, a media technician at the Destin City Library, for spending many hours with me capturing items digitally for display in this book. Your kindness and patience will not be forgotten.

Thank you also to my wife of thirty-three years, Susan, for putting up with another crazy idea of mine. You are always a rock for me. And finally, my two children, Cagney and Noah, who I hope one day will appreciate the effort to capture their great-grandfather's sacrifice in World War I.

BIBLIOGRAPHY

American Armies and Battlefields in Europe. Washington, DC: US Army Center of Military History, 1992.

American Heritage History of World War I. New York: American Heritage Publishing Co. Inc., 1964.

Barnett, Correlli. *The Swordbearers: Supreme Command in the First World War.* New York: William Morrow & Company, 1964.

The Editors of American Heritage, Narrative by S. L. A. Marshall. *The American Heritage History of World War I.* American Heritage Publishing Company, 1964.The 1982 edition is published by Bonanza Books, distributed by Crown Publishers, Inc., by arrangement with American Heritage Publishing Co. Inc.

History of the Sixth Engineers. New York: The Knickerbocker Press, 1920.

History of the Third Division United States Army in the World War (For the Period, December 1, 1917 to January 1, 1919). Cologne: Andernach-on-the-Rhine/Du Mont Schauberg, 1919.

GLOSSARY

Aeropla: Airplane

arr: Arrive

Aus: Australian

Bk. Bg: Barracks bag

Co: Company

Eng: English

I.O.O.F: International Order of Odd Fellows

J City: Jersey City

K.P.: Kitchen Patrol, or Kitchen Police. Soldiers were tasked to help prepare food and clean dishes for the kitchen staff.

O.Ds: Olive drab uniforms

Plat: Platoon

P.R.R.: Pennsylvania Railroad

Regt: Regiment

Sta: Station

Tommy: British soldier

YMCA: Young Men's Christian Association

NOTES

Chapter 1

1   *American Military History, Volume II: The United States Army in a Global Era, 1917–2003* (Washington, DC: Center of Military History, 2009), 7.

2   Howard Claypoole, Letter home to his parents, Mr. and Mrs. Winfield S. Claypoole, dated October 13, 1917.

3   Howard Claypoole, Letter home to his parents Mr. and Mrs. Winfield S. Claypoole, dated October 15, 1917.

4   Howard Claypoole, Letter home to his parents Mr. and Mrs. Winfield S. Claypoole, dated October 18, 1917.

5   Howard Claypoole, Letter home to his parents Mr. and Mrs Winfield S. Claypoole, dated November 5, 1917

6   *History of the Sixth Engineers* (New York: The Knickerbocker Press, 1920), 9.

Chapter 2

7   *American Military History*, 11.

8   George Cohan, "Over There" (New York: Leo Feist, 1917).

9   *History of the Sixth Engineers*, 256.

10   *History of the Sixth Engineers*, 7.

11   Ibid., 11.

12   Ibid., 49.

13   Ibid., 50.

14   William A. McGill, "USS *George Washington* Service, WWI and WWII," American Legion, April 10, 2018, https://www.legion.org/stories/my-time-uniform/uss-george-washington-service-wwi-and-wwii.

15   *History of the Sixth Engineers*, 52.

16   Ibid., 54.

Chapter 3

17   *History of the Third Division United States Army in the World War (For the Period, December 1, 1917 to January 1, 1919)* (Cologne: Andernach-on-the-Rhine/Du Mont Schauberg, 1919), xix.

18   *American Military History*, 11.

19   *History of the Sixth Engineers*, 30.

20   *American Heritage History of World War I* (New York: American Heritage Publishing Co. Inc., 1964), 267.

Chapter 4

21   "Second Battle of the Somme, 21 March–4 April 1918," https://www.historyof-war.org, accessed November 22, 2021.

22   *American Armies and Battlefields in Europe* (Washington, DC: Center of Military History, 1992), 25–26.

23   Correlli Barnett, *The Swordbearers: Supreme Command in the First World War* (New York: William Morrow & Company, 1964), 292.

24   *American Military History*, 28.

25   Ibid., 29.

Chapter 5

26   "World War I United States Military Records, 1917 to 1918," FamilySearch, https://www.familysearch.org/wiki/en/World_War_I_United_States_Military_Records,_1917_to_1918, accessed December 8, 2021.

27 Andrew Beckett and Edward J. Harvey, "Number 3 Canadian General Hospital (McGill) in the Great War: Service and Sacrifice," *Canadian Journal of Surgery* 61, no. 1 (February 2018): 8–12, https://dx.doi.org/10.1503%2Fcjs.012717.

28 Scott Harrah, "Medical Milestones: Invention of the X-Ray," University of Medicine and Health Sciences, November 5, 2014, https://www.umhs-sk.org/blog/medical-milestones-invention-x-ray.

29 Howard Claypoole, Letter home to his parents Mr. and Mrs. Winfield Claypoole, dated April 4, 1918.

Chapter 6

30 *American Heritage History*, 287.

31 Howard Claypoole, Letter home to his parents Mr. and Mrs. Winfield Claypoole, dated July 12, 1918.

32 *Swordbearers*, 335.

33 *American Heritage History*, 286.

34 Ibid., 285.

35 Ibid., 287.

36 *American Military History*, 38.

37 *History of the Sixth Engineers*, 94.

38 Ibid., 99.

39 Ibid.,104–105.

40 *American Military History*, 39.

41 Ibid., 26.

42 Howard Claypoole, Paybook, October 9, 1917–August 29, 1919.

43 Howard Claypoole, Letter home to his parents Mr. and Mrs. Winfield Claypoole, dated October 11, 1918.

Chapter 7

44 *American Military History*, 43–44.

45 *History of the Sixth Engineers*, 146.

Chapter 8

46 Ibid., 181.

47 Ibid., 179–80.

48 Ibid.,181.

49 Ibid., 186.

50 Ibid., 186.

51 Ibid., 187.

Appendixes

52 "Our Mission, Independent Order of Odd Fellows, https://odd-fellows.org/about/our-mission/, accessed November 29, 2021.

53 Fred L. Borch, "The Purple Heart—The Story of America's Oldest Military Decoration and Some Soldier Recipients," National Museum of the United States Army, https://armyhistory.org/the-purple-heart-the-story-of-americas-oldest-military-decoration-and-some-soldier-recipients/, accessed December 8, 2021.

```
        THE GREAT WAR
     THROUGH A DOUGHBOY'S EYES


            by


     Gregory S. Valloch
```

A good job, but one which needs far more
documentation, and research support.
The Amer. Heritage version is probably not the
best one. Official histories? und histories.
Specific + abstract comments on the diary.
You might have interleaved citations +
explanations in the diary text itself.
But you have a lot of good
material here and have
worked hard

Dr. Klinge
HI 300A
28 April 1983

A-/B+

THIS IS THE COVER SHEET FOR THE PAPER I WROTE FOR THE WORLD WAR I
CLASS TAUGHT BY PROFESSOR DENNIS KLINGE. WITHOUT THIS PAPER BEING
WRITTEN, THERE WOULD NOT BE A BOOK. FOR A COLLEGE STUDENT I PUT
A LOT OF WORK INTO THE PAPER AND IT CLEARLY EXCEEDED THE 15 PAGES
PROFESSOR KLINGE REQUIRED FOR THE CLASS. IT RAN TO 47 PAGES.